In Real Life

Love, Lies & Identity
in the Digital Age

Nev Schulman

GRAND CENTRAL
PUBLISHING

NEW YORK   BOSTON

Illustrations on pp. 91, 105, 123, 124, 130, 158, and 188 by Sean Donnelly (illus. on p. 188 based on original by Dallas Clayton). Photo on p. 100 by Max Joseph; photo on p. 115 by Michael Hart; photos on pp. 147 and 245 from the author's personal collection.

Grand Central Publishing
Hachette Book Group
237 Park Avenue
New York, NY 10017

www.HachetteBookGroup.com

Printed in the United States of America

RRD-C

First Edition: September 2014
10 9 8 7 6 5 4 3 2 1

Grand Central Publishing is a division of Hachette Book Group, Inc. The Grand Central Publishing name and logo is a trademark of Hachette Book Group, Inc.

The publisher is not responsible for websites (or their content) that are not owned by the publisher.

Library of Congress Cataloging-in-Publication Data has been applied for.

#IRLbook

To my grandparents,
Marvin, Phyllis, Lowell, Dianne, Toni, Marlene, and Hal,
for teaching me the importance of generosity, the value of humor,
and the meaning of family.

Contents

PART THREE
HOW TO LIVE AND LOVE OFFLINE, TOO

In Real Life

Introduction

It was 2:30 a.m. on an August night in 2008, and I was sitting in a rental car on a rural country road in Gladstone, Michigan. It was pitch black outside, with only one dim light illuminating a patch of yard, an empty horse trailer, and a barn. The girl I was falling in love with—a pretty young musician named Megan—was supposedly in that barn, helping a horse give birth to her foal.

At least, I *thought* she was someone I was falling in love with. The truth was, I'd never actually met her.

For eight months—ever since I'd encountered Megan online—she and I had been texting daily, spending hours on the phone every week, exchanging a huge volume of email and Facebook messages. We'd made attempts to get together—for me to visit her home in Michigan or her to come to me in New York City—but they'd all fallen apart for one reason or another. Still, we'd continued to grow closer, virtually befriending each other's friends and families. Even my mom loved Megan. I was in deep.

So why was I sitting in the car, silently freaking out? Why had I just engaged in a long debate with my brother, Rel, and my friend Henry, who had accompanied me there, about whether it made more sense to back into the farm's driveway (for a quick getaway) or drive in forward (so the headlights would illuminate the yard more)? Why was I not jumping out and running into that barn to finally see Megan, in the flesh, for the first time?

The answer to that question was way more complicated than I'd ever expected.

A few days before, I had discovered that Megan was lying about something—a seemingly small thing, but enough to raise a red flag. What else was she lying about? We'd had our first real fight. Rel, Henry, and I were in Vail, Colorado (where we were shooting a video) at the time, and decided to jump on a plane for a surprise visit to Michigan. I wanted to meet Megan once and for all so she could answer the questions that were starting to pop up in my mind.

What had started out earlier that day as an exhilarating, spontaneous trip grew more and more confusing the closer we got to Megan's farm. As we drove straight from the Chicago airport through Wisconsin, past Green Bay and along Lake Michigan, I had started to wonder: Was I headed for a thrilling encounter with real love, or a potential confrontation with a crazy person? The hours passed, and paranoia began to set in. Around midnight, we had stopped at Walmart to stock up on survival gear—bear spray and a case of bottled water, as if we were anticipating some sort of siege. Instead, our more optimistic and gentlemanly instincts took over, and we ended up buying presents for Megan and her family: CDs, a s'more-making kit, a ballet poster, and some dog toys for the family pet.

And now, finally, here we were. I was exhausted, yet high on adrenaline. I recognized the horse farm from the pictures Megan had sent me, so that was reassuring. When we opened the mailbox, just to confirm that someone named Megan actually lived there, we did find mail addressed to her. But it was mail *I* had addressed to her—some of it almost two months earlier. The postcards were stamped *Return to sender.*

Huh.

As Henry pulled the car into the driveway and then turned it around, I thought to myself, *This is the moment. This is the millisecond in the story of your life where you either go for it or don't. Either you walk up to that barn and your life potentially changes, or you flee.* And then, a more panicky internal voice: *If it's a horror movie, this is also the moment when you die.* But it wasn't a horror movie. It was real life. *My* life. And I knew that if I chickened out, I'd never get any answers at all.

Just do it.

I jumped out of the car, walked right up to the glass window of the barn door, and looked in.

———

If you are thinking right now that Megan probably didn't exist—you're right. I was about to be profoundly disappointed. It turns out I'd been "catfished"—a term that emerged out of the documentary that Rel, Henry, and I would make about my experience, and one that would quickly become a widespread meme encapsulating the growing phenomenon of online relationships based on fake identities. So, no—there was no Megan, at least not as I had known her. When I finally looked in that barn window, it was empty.

My experience trying to discern what had happened to me would end up becoming a documentary—*Catfish*—that would premiere at the Sundance Film Festival and turn out to be an international hit. It would spawn a TV show for MTV, in which I investigate online relationships to determine whether they are based on truth or fiction. (Spoiler: It's almost always fiction.)

Through all of this, I'd discover how universal my experience really was.

As we now know, "catfish" are everywhere. Every day stories turn up in the media—on *The View*, *Glee*, ESPN, *Vanity Fair*, and the *New York Times Magazine*, and those are just the ones that make it to the news. Thousands, maybe even tens of thousands of people are catfished every day. In the process of making *Catfish: The TV Show*, I've investigated dozens of these cases myself—and they don't even begin to scratch the surface. I receive hundreds of emails *every week* from people who believe they've been duped or are currently involved in a suspicious relationship.

Clearly, catfishing is an epidemic. But this book isn't just about being catfished.

The rise of catfishing has opened up the far bigger question of how we are living and loving in the era of social media. The vast majority of young people are now conducting their friendships and love affairs via social media, often (like me) with people they've never met in the flesh. Are you online? Then odds are you already know what I'm talking about: You've made friends, you've fallen in love, you've had *entire relationships* that never went past pixels on a screen.

There's always going to be a shortage of happiness. Thanks to Facebook and Twitter and Instagram and so on, we have a new way to search for the affection we crave. But far too frequently, we are engaging in Internet relationships—relationships that are founded on various forms of misrepresentation—*instead* of real-life relationships.

What I've learned in the course of making my documentary and TV show is that even though we have so many new ways of reaching out to one another, we don't know how to truly communicate anymore. We've distilled our interactions so that we don't have to deal with the sticky, complicated, uncomfortable reality that comes with expressing ourselves.

Instead of working our issues out, we fall back on white lies, half-truths, and downright dishonesty.

If you watch *Catfish: The TV Show*, you may sometimes feel frustrated by our brief explanations for some very complicated behavior. Well, where the TV show ends, this book really starts. Here I will dig into the deeper issues that motivate not just catfish, but everyone who spends significant time and energy on social media and their online relationships.

This book is for you if you find yourself looking at your smartphone fifty times a day instead of looking other people in the eye. Or if you find yourself worrying about your popularity online, obsessing over your profile photos, and counting your "likes." Or if you spend hours every day poring over Instagram posts and tweets, interacting with people you do not know, and disengaging from real life in order to stay connected to the online world.

This book isn't just for people who have been catfished—it's for *anyone* who lives online today.

Consider this an honest look at falling in love, loving yourself, and being loved in the social media age. It's a guide that addresses how to improve your actual life instead of living through your digital self.

We may all speak the same language, use the same emojis and acronyms, go to the same websites, but we've lost something important in the way we interact with one another.

We've replaced the spice of personal relationships—the benefits and burdens of being real—for the anonymity of social media; anonymity that allows us to create a persona free of the constraints of truth.

It's time to stop living *IRL*, and start living in real life.

PART ONE

Catfishing: A Primer

When I announced this book on my Facebook fan page, I asked my followers what they were most interested in reading about. I got hundreds of responses, ranging from "Tell us about your 'relationship' with your cameraman, Max" to "recovering from rejection" to "being so sexy it hurts 😘."

But by far the most common request was for more information about what you see on the show: You want a better understanding of who catfish are, why they do what they do, and what motivates them. What's the psychology behind catfishing? Why do catfish's victims believe every word they say? And how did *I* end up being hooked by a catfish?

This first section attempts to answer some of those questions. It reveals the complex reasoning behind some of the most bizarre stories we've uncovered. What does catfishing tell us about modern communication—and what does it say about us as individuals?

CHAPTER 1

My Catfish Story, Part One

The message that started it all arrived on a chilly December morning in 2007. I was at my new office on Broadway in Tribeca, a second-floor loft that I was sharing with Rel and Henry. The place was a disaster zone—boxes and papers and photographs and computer equipment everywhere. This small, chaotic space was home base for my videography and photography business and was where I worked as the media director for Morphoses / The Wheeldon Company, a new contemporary ballet troupe.

I probably should have been unpacking, or editing one of my many video projects, or—at the very least—cleaning up, but instead I was procrastinating. I'd already checked my Facebook profile a half dozen times when I decided to click over to Myspace, which I hadn't visited in months. There, I kept a fairly out-of-date profile under the title "Professional New Yorker."

In my Myspace inbox, I discovered a message, dated months earlier, from someone named "Abby Loves Ballet." It read, roughly:

Hi Mr. Schulman! My name is Abby. I'm 8 years old and live in Ishpeming, Michigan. I was in New York a few months ago on a trip with my mom. She took me to a performance of Morphoses. I saw your name on their web site and saw that you're a photographer. I really love your pictures. Anyway, since

I know you're a "professional New Yorker," I'd love to get your opinion on these paintings I just did of Central Park. I'm sure you're super busy. No worries if you don't have time to respond.

Peace and Love ~Abby

Later, I'd wonder whether the profile name Abby Loves Ballet had been created specifically to appeal to me and my love for dance, but at the time, I was charmed. Abby's profile picture was of a young girl with a big smile and long blond hair. *How funny and cute*, I thought. I clicked over to look at some of her paintings: They were pastel watercolor landscapes, mostly of trees and bridges in Central Park. I wasn't exactly a professional art critic, but I was sufficiently impressed. The paintings seemed pretty advanced for a kid her age.

It all seemed so genuine, which—after I'd lived my whole life in a city where cynicism is too often the default mode—came as a breath of fresh air. And I was flattered: It was the first time someone had reached out to tell me they were inspired by my photography.

I don't have the message that I sent back to her—my Myspace page is long gone—but as far as I can recall, my response went something like this:

Hey, thanks for your email. I checked out your paintings and they're really great. I particularly like the way you captured the light on the tree branches. Keep up the good work. Cheers.

And that was that. Or so I thought. Little did I know that she now had me on the hook. That one response would open a floodgate of more than 1,500 messages over the next nine months, and would ultimately change the direction of my entire life.

—————

As an eight-year-old girl living in a rural town in the Midwest, Abby was pretty much my polar opposite. I was a twenty-three-year-old native New Yorker, born, raised, and educated within twenty miles of Manhattan.

Let me give you some background.

My family's roots in the city run deep. My name, Nev, is short for Yaniv, the result of the time my parents spent in Israel before I was born. My dad's family, the Schulmans, are a Jewish family that emigrated from Eastern Europe in the late 1800s. My mother's family, the Baraschs, are also Eastern European immigrants. Both sides were dirt poor but hard workers, and they ultimately found success in New York: The Baraschs owned a deli in uptown Manhattan and the Schulmans were dressmakers in Scarsdale. My mom's father, Marvin, started an insurance company with his brother that he grew into one of the largest in the country. My dad's father became a wealthy real estate developer, a golf course designer, and one of the most respected figureheads in the Northeast golf community. My dad followed right in his footsteps.

My parents married young, after a very brief courtship, and soon after that my mom was pregnant with my brother, Rel. My parents' relationship was already strained when I was born three years later, and not long afterward they decided to part ways. I spent my childhood bouncing between my mom's apartment on the Upper West Side of Manhattan and my dad's house in Westchester (and then, after he moved, his apartment eight blocks south of my mom's).

My mom is a wildflower tomboy. I inherited my love of motorcycles from her. She's an original, passionate and impulsive. Her taste is eclectic, and her home is always beautiful. She loves to try new things: She worked as a florist, and then at the auction house Sotheby's, and finally as an event planner before going back to school to get her masters in social work. I love how creative and artistic she is, and she truly taught me the meaning of unconditional love. (I'll tell you more about that later.)

My dad is a passionate guy, always excited about something. He's also a total creature of habit. Every day, he wakes up at 4:45 a.m. He drinks two coffees, then attends two back-to-back Bikram yoga classes. He is compulsive, a real "all or nothing" kind of guy. I remember that for months at a time while I was growing up, he'd eat only peanut butter out of the jar with a spoon, and then one day he'd decide to never eat it again. He'd find a pair of pants he liked and buy ten pairs of them. He cleans constantly and is hypercritical—of me, of the women he dates, of himself. That's probably why he was a perpetual bachelor when I was growing up, and although he did fine for himself, he never seemed to be where he wanted to be.

I grew up worried that I'd struggle with the same issue: having a productive life and yet feeling that I'd settled for a lesser version of myself. (It remains a battle to this day. Every morning when I wake up, my head races with all the little things I have to do. It's a constant fight not to sweat the small stuff—the easy tasks within reach—and instead to focus on the bigger picture, to slowly work toward something even if it doesn't immediately produce results.)

Maybe it was because of my parents' early divorce (I'll save that question for the therapist), but at a breathtakingly young age, I was already a professional troublemaker. By the time I was six years old I'd been kicked out of kindergarten for intentionally clogging all the toilets and urinals with toilet paper. It was just the beginning of my long and illustrious career as a juvenile delinquent.

I lasted at my next school—a snooty uptown private school called Ethical Culture—for three years before I got in a tiff with a teacher about the length of my hair (too long) and then cursed out the principal. I wasn't invited back for fourth grade.

By the time I arrived at what is now called the Trevor Day School my parents had realized that my hyperactivity was diagnosable. ADHD was the buzzword of the moment. Ritalin became my new best friend, and for a while, things seemed to improve. I had a therapist, and my new school had smaller classrooms and a more visual curriculum that appealed to me. The National Dance Institute visited the school once a week to teach the students dance, and I discovered an aptitude for it. It was the first time I'd ever been good at something. It was NDI that introduced me to dance and gave me an outlet for much of the energy and creativity I was looking to express.

Still, I was wound up. I was constantly getting in fights with my brother: It would drive me crazy when he came home and threw his dirty socks on the floor. Plus, I had a lack of inhibition that was unusual for my age, and couldn't stop myself from trying to be the class clown. I never kept my mouth shut. In my freshman year of high school, I was suspended for procuring a condom from the bathroom's new condom dispenser and waving the unraveled prophylactic around in class. (My female classmates didn't think it was as funny as I did.)

But my real problem was stealing. I stole DVDs from Tower

Records, clothing from Ralph Lauren, and a host of other miscellaneous items. My attitude was, *If they're not doing a better job keeping an eye on it, it's their fault.* I hadn't yet learned accountability; I didn't understand that even if I wasn't personally dealing with the consequences of my actions, someone else was. And I got away with it until my senior year, when I stole a Wi-Fi card out of my computer teacher's desk. I was a rotten criminal: I didn't yet understand how IP addresses worked, and the offending card was quickly traced back to me. That was the end of my career at Day School. They gave me my diploma, but I wasn't allowed to attend the graduation ceremony with my class.

I managed to talk my way into Sarah Lawrence for college—or, to be more honest about it, my mother did the talking for me. As an active alumna, she used her clout to get me in. (Let's be blunt, she begged.) Once I landed at Sarah Lawrence, I promptly began getting myself into even more trouble. I broke into my dorm's basement and set it up as a subterranean party pad, throwing massive bashes. I snuck into a defunct restaurant in Yonkers and stole all their booze, kitting out my lofted dorm room with an epic bar. I sold weed and mushrooms.

Then there were the car crashes. Between 2002, when I was seventeen, and 2005, I wrecked a 1980 Porsche (fell asleep at the wheel), a Harley-Davidson (going too fast on vacation), and a 1992 Acura Legend (old lady stopped too suddenly in front of me), not to mention countless small skirmishes with my motorcycle on the rainy and snowy streets of Manhattan. It's probably a miracle I'm still alive.

I never thought of myself as lucky, though. Instead, I was cocky and arrogant and thoughtless. I remember breaking into the Sarah Lawrence cafeteria kitchen with friends one night: We put condoms between the sliced meats and I took a dump in the cereal dispenser—a stunt that shut down the kitchen for two days. (I can't believe I just admitted that.) Another time, I got revenge on an enemy who I'm pretty sure slashed the tires of my motorcycle by emptying a fire extinguisher in his closet and taking a number of his things. Even though I later felt guilty and returned his belongings in garbage bags, it took some serious convincing to get him to drop the damage charges against me. I can't say I blame him.

He wasn't the only one who hated me. I was on the outs with everyone. I disappointed my family; I infuriated authorities; I pissed off half the kids at school. I spent the better part of my life being told that I'd messed up and apologizing. I'd tell people that I understood what I'd done wrong, that I'd fix what I'd broken, that I'd do better next time—but I wouldn't. I didn't have any real friends because I couldn't be trusted. It's not that I was a bad person, but I didn't have any perspective. My actions were aggressive. My mantra was, "I do what I want." I took every risk that came my way. I rarely considered the consequences, and if I did, I either didn't understand the seriousness of the situation or thought I could handle it.

But despite my talent for spreading chaos, my appetite for risk allowed me to become a budding entrepreneur. My sophomore year, my brother, who was in film school, was offered a job filming a bar mitzvah. Not having time, he offered me the job. It was a two-thousand-dollar opportunity that I happily accepted, immediately employing my suitemate and filmmaker friend Thomas to coproduce with me. The video was a success and I was quickly referred to many other NYC clients. One of them asked if I knew a good event photographer, and without hesitation I suggested myself. Of course, I didn't have the proper experience or equipment, so when asked about my fee I simply researched what I'd need to buy and made that cost my quote. It worked: I had successfully bullshitted my way into being a professional photographer.

As the jobs kept coming in, I decided to take a year off from school to build a photography and videography business. I started a nightlife photography website called TheContactSheet .com, which quickly became a hit. I loved working and making money, and by the time I returned to Sarah Lawrence my junior year, my heart wasn't in school anymore (not that it ever really was to begin with). Not long after my return, I decided to photograph the school's annual Sleaze Ball, a night of debauchery, drugs, and girls dressed primarily in lingerie. While I was photographing, an individual who didn't like that I was taking pictures attempted to tackle me and smash my camera on the ground. Since the camera was attached to a strap around my neck, I found myself in a very unpleasant situation, much like a dog with a choke collar. In an effort to free myself, I punched the person and ran off; when I returned minutes later, I discovered that the short, stocky, crew-cut-styled individual that I'd fought with was a woman—a fact that I hadn't been aware of in the heat of the moment. The next thing I knew, I'd been arrested.

The case was dismissed almost immediately, but Sarah Lawrence took the opportunity to toss me out once and for all. I never even finished my junior year. My attitude was, "Never mind. No big deal. I had it coming." It didn't matter much to me. But my mom was crushed. She'd already put her neck out for me more times than I could count, and now I was hurting her legacy at the school she loved so much. I'd finally screwed up so badly that it ended her relationship with Sarah Lawrence for good.

The upside of leaving Sarah Lawrence was that I was able to get more involved in the ballet scene. Even though I wasn't planning to pursue a career on the stage itself, I loved being in that world, taking photos and going to events. My videography company was growing, too. I made event documentaries, wedding videos, dance films, and corporate promos. My photos appeared in major newspapers. A still from a ballet documentary that I was shooting—a male ballet dancer holding a female dancer aloft in the late afternoon sun—was printed on a half-page in the *New York Sun*.

By the time the winter of 2007 rolled around, I'd managed to move on from my troublemaker days (at least to the extent that I hadn't been arrested, gotten in a fight, stolen anything, or gotten thrown out of a school in three years—in my love life, I was still proving adept at making messes). I had carved out a seemingly good niche for myself in New York City. I was making enough money to live in my own apartment and pay the rent on that Tribeca office. I traveled when I felt like it, bought and sold old cars and motorcycles, and had an on-again off-again relationship with a dancer named Katie. I worked as little as I could in order to have as much fun as possible. I spent hours every day fiddling around with social media.

Honestly, though? I wasn't happy. My girlfriend was great, but she didn't trust me, and I wasn't ready for commitment. I had a business, but I wasn't particularly driven or passionate about it. I was frequently bored. I was underperforming, and I knew it. I sometimes thought of my dad and his chronic dissatisfaction, his palpable sense of disappointment with his life. Was I falling into the same patterns? I was capable of so much more. What was holding me back?

Instead of facing this head-on, I found myself constantly seeking out distraction. I took my mind off my issues by filling my life with small tasks and fun adventures. My goal on any given day was simply to convince myself I was enjoying life as best I could.

All this was festering on the December day that I received that first message from Abby. And although I wouldn't know it for many months to come, my vulnerable mental state was the reason I would end up getting pulled in so deep.

———

As far as distractions go, Abby turned out to be an A+. Almost immediately after I responded to her Myspace message, I received another Myspace message from someone named Angela Wesselman-Pierce:

> Hi there, I'm Abby's mom, Angela. I hope Abby's not bothering you. My son was babysitting her and he wasn't paying attention when she emailed you. My apologies.

I responded to let her know that I thought her daughter was charming, and that I was happy to engage with her. By the end of the day, I'd received a new message from Abby.

> One of my favorite photos of yours is the picture of the two dancers, the one that was in the New York Sun. Can I paint it and send it to you?

Of course, I replied. *You can use any of my photos that you want.*

And then:

Hi Yaniv!

Here's the deal, my Dad said he's ok with me painting from
your photos as long as I send the original to you or destroy the
original. I can't keep them or sell them because of my artistic
integrity and whatever so if that's ok with you it's ok with me.

I looked at some of your Photos and you have like a bazillion
photos that I would love to draw out! I also noticed that you
dance too...sweet. I think that officially makes you THE
Coolest person I've never met! And you have a Triumph?!
too sweet!

I'm sooo grateful to have heard from you today! I was afraid
my Mom was going to have me start drawing more old/dead
people today. It sooo much sucks being 8!!!

Peace and Love ~ Abby

A week later, a box arrived in the mail. When I opened it,
I found a meticulously rendered painting of my ballet photograph done in watercolor. It was surprisingly good. I figured
that Abby must be some kind of prodigy, and I felt flattered
that she was spending so much of her time and energy on me.
I framed the painting and put it on my desk. I enjoyed having
it in my office as a reminder of this interesting new twist in
my life.

Hey Abby, I like the drawing.

I would also love to have any of the drawings that you make
of my work.

More importantly, I would love to see you focus on some
of my movement photos.

I think it would be a good exercise for you to try and capture the energy of dance since you love it so much.

Please feel free to use any of my photos and to post the paintings/videos on your myspace or youtube or whatever.

- Cheers, Yaniv

By the end of January, I'd received a second box, full of paintings that Abby had modeled on my photographs as well as a few other odds and ends she wanted me to have: two really old dollar bills, a T-shirt from her brother's band, an old edition of *Macbeth*, some photographs she'd taken. I didn't even have enough wall space to hang all the paintings, so I kept them in a manila folder until I could frame them.

Rel and Henry were amused by the whole thing. The first paintings and the emails seemed as legit to them as they did to me, and they were intrigued enough to pull out their digital video cameras and film me opening the boxes. But they grew more skeptical as my inbox began to fill with long, chatty emails from Abby. And my girlfriend, Katie, was starting to express her distaste for my "eight-year-old girlfriend."

Initially, my correspondence was primarily with Abby—she would write me with cute rambling stories about her family, her art, her school, her pet rat. But soon I was spending as much time, or more, emailing with her mom, Angela. Our Myspace messages quickly moved into email exchanges, and within a month of Abby's first contact, Angela and I were emailing several times a week.

Angela struck me as being a pretty cool mom, direct and pleasant and funny. She was almost forty with two grown kids—Megan and James—as well as Abby, plus two teenage stepsons—the twins Alex and Anthony. She lived with her husband, Vince, in an old Victorian house in Ishpeming, a tiny town (population 6,470) in Michigan's rural Upper Peninsula. Everyone in her family seemed to have an artistic bent: The boys had a band, Megan was also a musician, and Abby was a painter. Angela herself was a psychologist and social worker, but she dabbled in art and music on the side. She'd once owned a small cafe and gallery called the House of Muses, but it had burned down in a fire. For a mom of five, she was remarkably put together: The photograph on her online profile depicted an attractive older woman with a long dark braid and dreamy eyes heavy with green eye shadow.

In her emails, Angela would ask me about my photography and tell me about her life in Ishpeming, about having kids younger than she'd expected, and about trying to encourage her kids' artistic interests. "We recognize that Abby has a lot of potential to do great things but we don't want to force those things on her," she'd write me. "I'm not a pushy Mommy that's trying to carve out some career for a child, those people scare me more than a little."

Soon, Angela and I were Facebook friends. In fact, she became Facebook friends with my mom, too! Entering Angela's Facebook world was like joining her family: Almost immediately, I was introduced to and "friended" by everyone linked to her profile. Unlike my four hundred–plus Facebook friends, Angela's Facebook circle was limited to less than two dozen friends and family members. There were the older kids, Alex, Anthony, and James; her husband, Vince; assorted cousins; a few of the kids' friends. There was Abby's babysitter, Noelle; the local art dealer, Tim Hobbins, who I was told was starting to sell Abby's work; and Ryan, Megan's best friend. I was fascinated by the dramatic and chaotic life of this family of hillbilly hippies. I loved feeling like I'd been included in this whole alternate community. It was such a curiosity, such a departure from my day-to-day existence.

The only person who *wasn't* on Facebook was Megan, Angela's nineteen-year-old daughter from a previous marriage. I'd been hearing about Megan since the very beginning of my correspondence with Angela and Abby. Megan was a musician and a dancer; she loved to ride horses; she had graduated from high school the previous year. She lived and worked in Lansing but came home on the weekends to be with her family. Abby adored her half sister.

Megan first appeared in my inbox a few weeks into my correspondence with Angela and Abby.

Hello Yaniv,

Our parents went away for a couple days and left my brothers and I to take care of Abby.

The last thing my Step dad said before he left was "What ever you do don't let Abby e-mail Yaniv Schulman anymore, she's bugging the crap out [of] him!" Welcome to my world bawahahahaha! (that's my evil laugh) A word of advice, don't give Abby [your] cell number or she'll text you to death. She's the reason everyone in the family gets unlimited texting and our parents still pay our cell phone bills. She can be quite chatty, I'm sure you've noticed.

The reason I'm e-mailing you now is I need to know what Abby's painting next. Abby's about finished with the 18x24 painting of the woman in the field of flowers and she's getting ready to pick her next project. You mentioned "movement photos", what photos specifically are you referring to? If the paintings [were] going to end up in the fireplace I suppose it wouldn't matter but since she's sending them to you it makes sense to me if you're going to end up with the paintings you should be the one to pick the subject.

Thank you for being so kind to my sister, you're a Sweetheart!

Enjoy your New Years Eve!

-Megan

Megan's emails were sporadic in the beginning, but by mid-February we were emailing at least once a week, chatting mostly about Abby's artwork, but also increasingly about Megan's life with her extended family—about dogsledding and ballet classes and horseback lessons and trips to Washington. She told me a tragic story about the sudden death of Abby's best friend, Danny, the previous summer—a congenital heart defect had triggered a heart attack, and he died in Abby's arms. I was touched. Megan seemed like a really sweet girl; her life in the country seemed enchanted.

Intrigued, I asked Megan why she wasn't on Facebook. "I've had my fair share of weirdness come from posting my pictures on Myspace and Facebook," she responded (a comment that I would later find very ironic).

Finally, in early March, more than three months after my initial email from Abby, I received a Facebook friend request from someone named Megan Faccio. The profile picture was of a stunningly pretty girl with big blue eyes, long blond-streaked hair, and a coy smile.

I friended her back instantly. And that's when things started to get serious.

CHAPTER 2

What Is a Catfish?

If you're reading this book, you probably already know what a catfish is. But for those of you who are new to the whole concept (in which case—Hi! Nice to meet you!), here's the UrbanDictionary.com definition:

> A catfish is someone who pretends to be someone they're not, using Facebook or other social media to create false identities, particularly to pursue deceptive online romances.

Maybe it's easiest to define *catfish* with a good story.

Let's start with Manti Te'o, a promising linebacker at the University of Notre Dame. For nearly a year, starting in 2011, he was in an online relationship with a pretty Stanford student named Lennay Kekua, who had befriended him through Facebook and Twitter. They had never met in person—after all, they lived halfway across the country from each other— but they spoke on the phone several times a day, so often that Te'o considered Lennay his girlfriend.

In the summer of 2012, Lennay called to tell Te'o that she'd been in a car accident, and as a result of her hospitalization, the doctors had discovered that she had undiagnosed leukemia. Despite bone marrow transplants, by mid-September Lennay was dead. A few days after getting this news, Te'o went out and scored a triumphant victory against Notre Dame rival Michigan State. Afterward, he told the sports media that Lennay's tragically premature death had inspired him to win. It made a great story—until the media did some digging and discovered that Lennay didn't exist, except as a Twitter and Facebook profile. There was no Stanford student, no car accident, no tragic battle with cancer. Instead, "Lennay" was a twenty-two-year-old boy named Ronaiah Tuiasosopo who'd been deceiving Manti all along.

It was a textbook catfishing case, and the mainstream media went nuts for it, with coverage everywhere from ESPN to *Vanity Fair*. You would have thought Te'o was the first person who had ever been duped in that way. But the truth is that since some caveman told the very first lie thousands of years ago, people have been pretending to be someone they're not, frequently in the name of romance. (Look at the themes of many Shakespeare plays and you'll see that identity deception has been a part of our culture for a while.) The difference today is that the Internet has made this much, much, *much* easier. Now, if you want to be a blond fashion model or a race-car driver or a Stanford student with a winning smile, you can be: All you need to do is find a photo, put up a Facebook page, and voila.

And in fact, that's exactly what's happening, over and over, in America and around the world. Catfish stories like Te'o's (and my own) are popping up with increasing frequency, and not just on my TV show. Consider this: Facebook admits that a mind-boggling 83 million Facebook profiles—8.7 percent of all profiles—are fakes or dupes. That's a lot of people who don't actually exist, conducting online relationships as if they are real people. This culture of deceptive online identity has grown so much that even social media profiles that *are* legitimate are increasingly riddled with lies.

In other words, catfishing has become so ingrained in modern life that many people do it unconsciously, in small but significant ways.

Even among those who set out to intentionally create a fake new identity, not all catfish are the same. Catfish tend to fall into a number of different categories, from fairly benign to incredibly malevolent.

Let's break them down, shall we?

CYRANO CATFISH

If you didn't learn the story of Cyrano de Bergerac in English lit—or see the movie *Roxanne*—here's a quick recap: Seventeenth-century poet with alarmingly large nose who believes he is unworthy of love agrees to help his handsome friend woo the beautiful Roxanne, whom Cyrano is also in love with, by writing her beautiful love letters for him. The Cyrano catfish takes that classic story and gives it a digital twist: Instead of love letters, it's Facebook messages, and instead of a handsome friend as a stand-in, it's a fake profile.

Of all the catfish I've encountered, these are by far the most common: people who seek, or unintentionally find, love under false pretenses. Cyrano catfish are generally insecure about themselves—their looks, their lives, their families, their jobs—and so they create fake profiles for the people they *wish* they were. And as those fake people, they have online romances.

Some of these catfish set out—as Cyrano did, and as Ronaiah Tuiasosopo also did—intending to fool someone specific. But they do so because they want to connect with another person. Others stumble into relationships accidentally. They don't set out to deceive someone in the pursuit of romance. Instead, they create their fake social media profiles as a coping mechanism for their feelings of isolation and loneliness, their insecurity and fear. In other words, they're trying to escape their problems via an idealized version of themselves. They think that under this new, more attractive guise, they will be appreciated for who they "really are" rather than being judged for how they look, or where they live, or the size of their bank account. They just want to be liked. Unfortunately, those fake profiles engage with real people. And the next thing you know, they are involved in a deceptive online relationship.

Take, for example, the case of James (episode 110), a guy who decided to reinvent himself in order to escape a less-than-exciting life and a criminal charge that had been dropped but was still associated with his name online. His Internet alter ego was Ja'Mari, a model and inspirational speaker with five thousand followers. Ja'Mari was who James felt he *could* be, if only he didn't have all his baggage. As Ja'Mari, James connected with Rico, a gay National Guard member, and what started as a friendship snowballed into a serious online relationship. Although James hadn't created Ja'Mari in order to ensnare Rico, when Rico found out about the deception, he was still hurt.

Cyrano catfish like James often know that what they are doing isn't exactly kosher. But that doesn't stop them from doing it. They need it. It gives them happiness, some sort of positive reinforcement, and the distraction from their lives that they crave.

REVENGE CATFISH

The revenge catfish is a different kind of beast. This is someone who sets up a fake profile not because they are looking to genuinely connect with a new person, but because they want to get back at someone they already know. The intention from the get-go is to deceive and hurt somebody.

A good (if complicated) example is the story of Mhissy (episode 104). Mhissy had a brief relationship with a girl named Jasmine. After Jasmine ended the relationship, Mhissy went on to date an ex-boyfriend of Jasmine's. When Jasmine, who was now pregnant, contacted her ex-boyfriend to request a paternity test, Mhissy, who was still pissed at Jasmine, got mad. (Like I said: complicated.) Instead of talking to Jasmine about it, Mhissy set up a fake profile of a handsome man and started flirting with Jasmine with the intention of distracting her from her ex-boyfriend and messing with her mind. It worked, for a crazy long time.

BENEVOLENT CATFISH

In rare cases, a catfish can set up a profile with the specific purpose of trying to help someone. I've only come across a few, but here's a good example:

Gladys (episode 201) had been best friends with Cassie since grade school. When Cassie's father was murdered, her life began a downward spiral—she began drinking heavily, doing drugs, and sleeping around. Gladys, desperate to stop Cassie's self-destructive behavior, created a fake profile of a handsome guy and friended Cassie. Over the course of two years, Cassie's new online boyfriend—and eventual fiancé—"Steve," helped build up her self-esteem and pull her out of the darkness. Gladys even enlisted her male cousin to be the voice of the fake boyfriend (going so far as to have phone sex with Cassie).

Of course, Cassie wasn't exactly thrilled to learn that she'd been lied to—the phone sex in particular was pretty horrifying to her—but she at least understood that Gladys had undertaken this whole deception with the best intentions.

Another fascinating benevolent catfish story that I investigated (but that never aired) started with a girl who couldn't get her deadbeat ex to pay his child support. Instead, she reached out to his even more recent ex-girlfriend for help, and the two of them collaborated to form a third, fake girl with the intention of using her to convince him to pay child support. (Yes, I know that some of these stories are convoluted. That's what real life is like.) Together, they made the girl that they knew he'd think was perfect—and it worked! She flirted with him, got him to talk about his daughter, told him she hoped he was "really supportive" of her, and otherwise massaged him into believing that the right thing to do was become a more financially responsible guy.

It all worked beautifully until he figured out that the girl in the pictures was actually another girl—at which point the two girls who started it all had to reach out to *that* girl, and got her to participate in the ruse! Next thing you know, girl number three was video-chatting with the deadbeat dad as the fake girlfriend, too.

SWINDLING CATFISH

Swindling catfish are the ones that I personally have the hardest time relating to. For these catfish the exchange that takes place with their victim isn't for affection or attention, but for their livelihood. The swindling catfish's goal is to scam people for cash, or more.

This kind of stuff happens every day online (in fact, these types of swindles pre-date the Internet), and stories about it are becoming increasingly common. The most frequent story you'll hear is about men who get involved online with "women" from foreign countries and send cash to them for plane tickets or moving expenses, only to get stood up. Perhaps the most widely known case—featured on the cover of the *New York Times Magazine* last year—involved a world-renowned particle physicist who got involved with a Czech "bikini model" on an online dating site and flew to Bolivia to meet her. She had allegedly just left for a modeling job in Argentina, but asked him to bring her the suitcase she'd left behind. The suitcase was full of drugs, and the physicist was subsequently arrested. He has spent the past few years rotting in jail in Argentina.

Most of the catfish I encountered on the first two seasons of the show were people who believed that a false online personality was the best way to sort through some emotional confusion or an identity crisis they were having, rather than just trying to steal from others. But in season three, I encountered more of these Swindling catfish, people who created false identities with the intention of deception for their own material or financial gain. If you're going to get hooked, this is the worst kind of person to have on the other end.

CELEBRITY IMPERSONATORS

Then there are the all-too-common impersonating catfish, who pretend to be celebrities online. Even I've been a victim of this scam: Do a search for my name on Facebook and you'll come across more than thirty profiles claiming to be Nev Schulman, including a profile just for my chest hair. (Yes, it's exceptionally lush, but come *on*.) One of these profiles had 4,500 followers before it was shut down; the catfish who ran it was chatting with his "friends" every day as me.

Sometimes these impersonators are a type of Cyrano catfish (think Keyonnah and Bow Wow in episode 214), but usually they are caught up in the currency of having "fans," and they derive a strange emotional satisfaction from driving up their numbers, despite the fact that the whole thing has nothing to do with them.

The truth is, it's not just celebrities who are impersonated. Think about all those Facebook friends you have that you've never met. They have access to all of your information. They could be on your profile right now, downloading your photos and creating another *you* somewhere else in order to catfish someone. It's scary how easy it is to impersonate someone and how casually a catfish can damage the reputation of the person they're pretending to be.

Which brings me to...

EVERYONE ELSE

The fact is, there are catfish everywhere you go on the Internet. Anyone who has dated online has surely encountered profiles that use photoshopped or altogether false pictures and contain fudged information. That cute doctor you chatted with for weeks but never actually met? The hot exotic dancer who bailed on you three times because she had to work? There's a fair chance they were catfish.

Looking out at the Internet landscape, it's clear that false identities, from the mild prevarication to the jaw-dropping lie, have come to pervade every part of online life. A lot of people think that the catfish phenomenon is just a popular scam, just a digital deception. But in my experience, the issue of catfishing is so much deeper and more complex than that. It's the most extreme symptom of a trend in society away from the honesty and confidence that a face-to-face relationship demands and toward the isolation and cowardice of online connections. It's about the insecurity at the center of online life. About the fear of a real life lived in public that drives people to decide that it's better to pretend to be someone else entirely. About the way we *all*—catfish or not—curate ourselves online to be "better" or more "interesting" than we really are, presenting images and ideas that don't align with our real selves.

The rise of false online identities has opened up the bigger question of how social media is shaping both our romantic relationships and the way we function in our day-to-day lives. What is it about social media that compels us to lie? What happens when online relationships are based on small fictions or big deceptions; when *everyone*, intentionally or not, is participating in a culture of false identity? In a world where human interaction takes place through a screen, how do we learn to be honest and to trust that others are, as well?

CHAPTER 3

Fishing for Compliments:
What Motivates Catfish?

What's *wrong* with those people?"

I hear this a lot about catfish. It's usually said in a dismissive tone: *those* people.

Since I've already touched briefly on the motivations of each type of catfish by defining the categories, I'm going to use this chapter to dig into what drives the most common type of catfish: the Cyrano.

You may wonder: What on earth would possess someone to pretend to be someone else and then get involved in a long-term online relationship, knowing full well that they can never meet the person they are "with" without blowing their cover? Anyone who does that must just be a crazy freak. Or so a lot of people think.

In my experience, it's not that simple. In fact, the motivations of your average catfish are both incredibly complicated and also far more relatable than you might expect. Often, there's nothing unusual or crazy about them at all—it's just that they use the Internet as an outlet for their issues in a way that other people don't (that is, in place of a therapist).

Let's start with a story.

A teenage girl named Kristen (episode 207) is in a terrible car accident. She loses one of her eyes and is bedridden for months. Her boyfriend dumps her. Her friends stop visiting. She gains weight. And then there's the matter of her glass eye, about which she's very insecure. She looks nothing like the person she used to be. She's miserable and lonely.

So what does she do? She creates a fake online persona, a version of the girl she wishes she still was. She keeps the details of this alternate "Kristen's" life similar to her own—the accident, her current enrollment in beauty school—but she changes her last name to disguise herself and swaps out her photos for those of a pretty acquaintance she feels she used to look like. It feels good to have people treat her normally again; cathartic; a relief. And using this new profile, she meets a boy on Facebook named Mike. They become friends, first talking on Facebook and then on the phone, ultimately speaking almost every day. He talks her off a ledge when she feels like ending it all. Soon, she feels like she's in love; she's totally emotionally dependent on Mike. By this point, Kristen is too afraid to reveal herself, knowing full well that if she does, Mike may reject her.

So she keeps up the charade. Until the day we show up at her door with Mike in tow and the whole thing falls apart.

So—what motivates these catfish? Typically, it's the same thing that motivates just about everyone: the desire to be liked and accepted. Usually, it's coupled with a sense of isolation. Insecurity. Depression. A negative self-image. So while your average catfish may not be a "crazy freak," they almost always have serious issues they need to work out. Most could probably use some therapy. (I speak from experience here: I've dealt with many of these issues myself, and since a very young age I've been lucky enough to see therapists regularly. Despite the cultural stigma against therapy, I honestly don't think I'd be where I am today if it hadn't been for my shrinks and their objective advice.)

Cyrano catfish create the version of themselves that they would like to be in order to see what kind of attention they would get if they were that person. It's easier than losing the weight (too daunting and sometimes not possible because of health issues), or going to college (not affordable or practical), or getting that great job (easier said than done). These catfish want to know what it would feel like to transcend their own issues. Often, their victims are collateral damage along the way.

I've encountered countless catfishing cases during the past few years, and every single one is unique (some are so complicated and convoluted that they're hard to even synopsize coherently), but I've come to recognize that there are a couple recurring themes. Personal issues that come up again and again. Every catfish may be distinct, but the root of their behavior often stems from the same place.

APPEARANCE

Yeah, it's a cliché, but it's true. The person behind that picture of an implausibly beautiful, skinny girl? In all likelihood, she's unhappy about her weight. Or maybe she just doesn't meet the impossible standards of beauty that society projects in ads, magazines, and movies, and is insecure about it. And that guy who claims to be a "male model" whose photos show six-pack abs? Yeah, right. Trust me: He's not so built in real life. A good third of the catfish who appear on the show have body-size issues or some deep-rooted concern about how they look that makes them miserable. (I can relate to that misery, since I myself suffer from the same affliction. Most notably about my build and body hair. Though I've come to love the way I look, it's nothing like the hairless pumped-up dudes I see in underwear ads and in movies.)

This is a symptom of our culture's obsession with appearance; our confusion about what beauty is and how we should feel about our bodies; and our compulsion to compare ourselves to the people we see on TV and on social media. Beauty is internal—related to energy and confidence—but we rarely remember this. Instead, most people, no matter their size or appearance, seem to feel like they've come up short. For catfish, that's often a trigger that sets off the lies.

Take, for example, Melissa, a girl I met in the first season of *Catfish* (episode 105). She had an unhappy life: At home she had a troubled relationship with her stepfather, and at school she was bullied for being overweight. Her self-esteem had bottomed out. But she discovered that on the Internet she could be thin and pretty! And when she was thin, people were nice to her! So she created a fake profile for a skinny blonde named Abby, met a guy named Jarrod, and the rest is *Catfish* history.

The ugly truth is that the world is often downright cruel to both women and men who are heavier. This nastiness can do a number on someone who is already suffering from a lousy self-image. When somebody absorbs that much negativity, it's no wonder they feel unlovable the way they are. Pretending to be a more conventionally attractive person on the Internet helps that person get the validation and attention they crave. It's easy to believe that once all our physical issues are hidden away, we'll be liked for being "ourselves." A new persona also makes it a lot easier to avoid having to face up to internal unhappiness.

Of course, all this serves as a distraction from resolving the real issues at play. Rather than getting up from their computer, taking a walk, and trying to improve their health or change their appearance, a person who is unhappy about their weight often uses the validation of their fake profile to avoid the issue altogether. This only drives the self-dissatisfaction further.

SEXUALITY

If appearance is the number one issue that leads to catfishing, sexuality is a close second. Another third of the catfish stories that I investigate involve men and women who are gay, bisexual, or transgendered. In many parts of the United States—not to mention vast swaths of the rest of the world—people are still closed-minded, and it's just not considered acceptable to come out as gay. Even in more liberal communities, a lot of gay kids have families that won't accept them.

Kids who grow up being taught that their homosexuality is wrong often turn to the Internet. There, they can flirt or even have "sex" with the same sex, using false identities, and no one will know. It's a stealthy and supposedly risk-free way to experiment with something that they are afraid to reveal to their (often religious) families and communities; to "sin" without really sinning, and to do it anonymously.

On the Internet, a confused gay kid can also find an outlet for feelings that he or she may not yet understand or know how to act upon. Kids who are bullied or are outcasts because of their sexuality can try on different identities in order to be accepted; maybe they even think that they can only be "loved" if they step into the persona of the opposite gender.

Take, for example, Aaron, whom I met in our first season (episode 108). As a gay high school sophomore living in small town Michigan, he set up a profile of a pretty blond girl named Amanda and spent the next five years deceiving straight guys online. "It feels better than being myself," he told us. "I realized other people had problems with me being gay, but when I went to Amanda I could convince a straight guy to like my personality. I don't want to be gay, but that's something I can't change." What he *could* change, thanks to social media? He could "be" a straight girl, rather than a gay guy, and play out his sexual interests in a more socially acceptable way. As Amanda, he could meet the guys he was too embarrassed to try to date in person.

Unfortunately, none of these relationships could ever materialize in real life, so they were doomed from the start.

CONTROL

It should come as no shock that a lot of catfish are people who feel like they have no control in their lives. Take Alicia, a twenty-three-year-old we met in the second season (episode 211). She was unemployed, physically unfit, and had been taken advantage of by a previous boyfriend. Her life was rudderless. So she began starting fake relationships online—in our case, with a girl named Aaliyah. Alicia pretended to be a lesbian in order to get Aaliyah "to fall in love with [her] and buy [her] things." Although at first this seemed like a swindling catfish case, there was more to it. Alicia had been hurt by life. At the heart of the matter was that instead of feeling out of control, she could be *in* control.

When they become catfish, previously helpless people suddenly feel like they are masterminds. From behind their alternate personae, they can manipulate the people around them; they can provide their characters with all the successes that they themselves lack. It gives them a sense of accomplishment and power that they can't seem to locate in their real lives.

Until, that is, they are exposed and the whole facade crumbles.

FEAR

No duh, right? Hiding behind a fake profile is a pretty good sign that someone is terrified of being themselves. But let's break it down further.

People who catfish are, for the most part, very fearful people. They are afraid of rejection. Something about who they are—their looks, their background, their home—strikes them as being unlovable. And so rather than risk their hearts in real life, they hide behind online profiles and digital barriers.

Take Derek, a guy we met in the second season (episode 204). For eight years he'd been chatting with a girl named Lauren, but he refused to video-chat or meet up with her in person. He wasn't pretending to be someone he wasn't or hiding some kind of physical issue, but he understood that in the real world, relationships often don't work out. And what he had online with his dream girl seemed so good that he didn't want to risk it falling apart. Simply put, he was scared.

And in a way, he was right. If you do make an emotional connection with someone online, what are the chances that you'll also have physical chemistry in person? If you aren't physically attracted, after all, it doesn't matter how much you like someone: It's just not going to work romantically. That was Derek's fear; it's the fear of almost all catfish. They're afraid that the magic they've found online will suddenly come to an end once they expose their true selves.

Even though there's a logic to this fear, the outcome is that some people never make that leap or take that chance; instead they end up living half a life. (The good news for Derek? We finally brought him face-to-face with Lauren, and they ended up falling in love for real and getting engaged. And subsequently breaking up. But hey, at least they gave it a chance. As Alfred Lord Tennyson wrote, it's "better to have loved and lost than never to have loved at all.")

Fear helps no one—not the catfish, and not the person whose feelings they are toying with.

ADDICTION

Imagine this: A catfish creates a whole new persona and unleashes it on the world. They have essentially given birth to a digital human being, an alternate version of themselves who is out there, engaging with other human beings. The catfish is responsible for the life of their creation, much like they would be for a pet or a child.

A lot of people find that very fulfilling. They think, "I've created this mini-me that people *like*. I can take care of him, send him on exotic trips, make him a model. My creative, artistic spawn can make other people happy!"

For a while, it does. But meanwhile, this digital creation's relationships are starting to get *demanding*. The fake person is connected with real people who expect responses to their messages. His profile needs constant maintenance and nurturing. It starts to snowball. The people he's talking to have real emotions, and things get complicated. The responsibility to the profile gets out of control. How does the catfish prevent someone who is passionately involved with this mini-me from coming to visit? They have to invent increasingly elaborate lies.

Catfish become hostages to their own creations, like Dr. Frankenstein. They may have breathed life into these digital personas, but now their monsters control them. It becomes a self-inflicted addiction. They don't feel they have a choice: Either they keep going, or they have to kill off the profile. And since they feel like their profile is a version of themselves, they are hesitant to murder their digital babies. They are hooked, and it escalates until it's completely out of control.

FANTASY

There's one common denominator that I've noticed in almost every catfish I've encountered over the past few years: an active fantasy life. Catfish use the Internet to fantasize the life they *want* into existence, in order to avoid dealing with the life they actually have.

Take Felicia, a season 1 catfish (episode 111). In her online relationship with Mike, she used real pictures of herself, but she changed many of the major details of her life. Instead of admitting that she lived in Orlando, where she was attending school, she told Mike that she lived in Jersey City and ran a salon that was in Orlando—which was her actual life goal.

Her online persona was simply a kind of projection, spinning out the life she hoped to live someday.

Many catfish we meet are doing some version of the same thing: imagining their desired lives into existence. "I'm a model!" "I travel a lot!" "I have a great big house and a nice car!" (You'd be amazed how critical a nice car seems to be.) They trump up their life accomplishments; they say they are attending college when they're not—but they *want* to be. Some are acting out extremely unrealistic versions of their lives, while others—like Felicia—are drawing a new life for themselves that's almost within reach.

You could argue that manifestation is a powerful tool, that envisioning your goals is the first step toward making them real. Unfortunately, the fantasy aspect of social media often gets in the way of real progress. Social media has come along and said, "You don't have to take real steps to actualize your dreams at all! You can 'have' the fantasy right now!"

Pretending online that you're living your dream life is free, it's immediate, and you're the only one who knows the truth. And yet, pretending to be successful is *not* the same as being successful.

So what motivates catfish, ultimately, is being unmotivated. The things they want—to feel good about their appearance, to be successful, to be lucky in love, to live the life they long for—are only achievable if they go out and make them a reality. But they don't. Instead, they hide behind fake profiles, "live" out their fantasies online, and let their day-to-day existence remain unsatisfying. The Internet is just an escape; the personal issues that have triggered their behavior will not go away until they step away from the computer and start dealing with real life.

CHAPTER 4

Hook, Line, and Sinker: Why People Fall for Catfish

All right. By this point, you probably get the modus operandi of your typical catfish. You know what makes them tick. But what about their victims? The people who buy into their hoaxes? What kind of person would fall for a deception that often looks mind-bogglingly obvious from the outside? Or are these "victims" even really victims? It takes two to catfish, after all.

I am probably one of the best-equipped people to answer that question. After all, I *am* that person. I was, as we put it, "on the hook" for nine months.

So why was I such a sucker? And how can people still be falling for this even after my show has been on the air for the past three years?

First of all, there are catfish, and then there are *catfish*. What I mean is that some catfish make eye-rollingly transparent claims (see: anyone who says they're an underwear model), but others can be extremely sophisticated liars. I managed to get involved with the latter. My catfish was creative, even sending me genuine newspaper stories that referenced (or seemed to reference) stories she'd told me. She set up Facebook profiles for at least fourteen people, ultimately building an incredibly complicated network of fake people that seemed, from where I sat in New York, to be totally real. She even had my mom convinced on a very personal motherly level. And if some of the stories that Megan, Angela, and Abby told me seemed amazing, who was I to know what life in rural Ishpeming, Michigan, was like? It was so radically distant from my urban New York life.

The nail in the coffin of my gullibility? The five hundred dollars I received in the mail, money that the family had promised me as a result of my influence on Abby's work. They wanted to pay me a cut of her painting sales, since those paintings were mostly based on my photos. Why on earth would these people have sent me that check if there wasn't a legitimate sale of a painting? And if that was the case, the whole story—about a child art prodigy; her goofy, fascinating family; and her alluring, flirtatious older sister—had to be true.

But even *that* doesn't really answer the hard question of why I became a victim. Looking back, there were plenty of red flags that I didn't pay attention to. Honestly, the main reason I chose to believe in my catfish's lies? It wasn't how convincing my catfish was. It was all about what was going on inside *me*. I chose to believe. I *wanted* to believe.

It's time for some more backstory.

At the time that Megan and I began to correspond, I was searching for something. I didn't know what it was, but I'd been searching for it for years. Sure, I'd started my production company with my brother at age nineteen and had built it into a reasonably profitable business, but did I want to be making bar mitzvah videos for the rest of my life? Hardly.

I also had a very light work schedule, to say the least—some weeks working twenty hours or less—so I had a lot of free time that I didn't know what to do with. I spent some of that time working on a photography event website—mostly shooting ballet parties and performances—as an attempt to reach out and be part of that community. But overall, I wasn't spending my time very productively.

My identity at that point in my life was heavily tied to my sexuality. That's where I drew my confidence; that's how I identified myself. I was a flirt. I was charming. And since I wasn't particularly fulfilled in my work life, I overcompensated by spending my time pursuing women. I got my sense of accomplishment from dating girls I wanted to date and sleeping with girls I wanted to sleep with. I was using my sexuality as a crutch. As a result, I had no shortage of relationships with women, but I couldn't ever seem to make them work. Big shock, right?

I wanted attention. A sense of value. I wanted to be needed. I'd go to parties, take pictures, get laid. But it wasn't fulfilling. It was surface. It was "lite."

And making matters worse, I'd recently made a lot of really lousy decisions. I'd been kicked out of college; ruined my relationship with my best friend, Mark, by hurting him badly in a fistfight (more on that later); and had a falling-out with my brother. I didn't like myself. I was disappointed, frustrated, lazy, and underaccomplished. I knew I could be doing so much more, but I felt stuck. And I knew that people didn't like me much, either. I had developed a reputation for being a rule breaker, a flirt, a loose cannon, and kind of a dick. I was not a particularly reliable guy.

Into this gaping chasm stepped—or, I should say, *typed*— Abby, Angela, Megan, and the rest of the Ishpeming crew. Here was a creative and passionate family who said that their budding young artist admired me and drew her inspiration from me. For the first time in my life, I genuinely felt a sense of value: Something pure and meaningful and lovely was happening as a result of my existence! I was thrilled to be part of this exciting exchange. I was thrilled that they appreciated my photos.

Better yet, it was an opportunity to start totally fresh, with a clean slate. They knew nothing of my life in New York City, my past fuckups. All they did was admire me. I could build a version of myself the way I'd *like* to be (sound familiar?), with new people who had no connection to my family or friends or where I lived. It was the ultimate reinvention—and, though I didn't know it at the time, a close cousin to what my catfish was doing.

As a bonus, Megan was a great new distraction, an outlet through which I could channel all my frustration and excess energy. It was fun! Instead of pursuing girls in New York, or working on my relationships, or building my company, I had a new hobby—a potential virtual romance with this beautiful Renaissance woman who admired me.

The people I've met who have been catfished (on the show, we call them *hopefuls*) have similar stories to mine. They have an almost universal desire to improve themselves. To be "seen" in a new and more flattering light, to be respected and admired based on their personalities and not their past actions. It's why so many people get easily lured into these online relationships. They don't see a lot of value in themselves. They are struggling to identify what makes them happy. And then along comes this person online who shows them that they *are* valuable. (And that's usually how it works. You are approached: The catfish *chooses* you. A random stranger contacts you and says, "I like the way you look and the photos you post, and I want to tell you that I appreciate you." And you're hooked.) The catfish seems to get something meaningful out of communicating with the hopeful, and it gives the hopeful a sense of importance. At the beginning, at least, it's a symbiotic relationship.

It also feels like a very safe environment. Not only is the hopeful physically removed from the person they're communicating with, but they have the ability to perfectly curate how they are perceived. The words they type, the photos they post, how quickly they respond—all of it feels very controllable. The hopeful can show this new "friend" all of the good stuff and none of the bad.

That was certainly the case for me with Megan, Abby, and Angela. I thought I could put all the negative stuff away in a box—the hypersexuality, the lack of focus, the general dickishness—and work on trying to be the good person I *hoped* to be. I was attempting, through this relationship with them, to begin to identify how I could be a better version of myself. I was carefully controlling everything I told them. I was so in love with this idea of the new, improved me that I was totally blind to what was really going on.

Thinking about it now, I realize how similar my motives for *being* catfished were to the motives of a catfish. Hopefuls and catfish are, more often than not, simply two sides of the same coin.

———

So that's why *I* was emotionally vulnerable to a catfish. Most other catfish victims tell a variation of the same story: the insecurity, the lack of focus in their lives, the desire to be appreciated and to improve themselves. After all, no one gets hooked because they are stable, are in great relationships, and have their lives together. Instead, they tend to need something emotionally that the catfish provides.

Consider the unforgettable story of Ramon, a nineteen-year-old guy living an unfulfilling life in Bullhead City, Arizona (episode 203). His parents were divorced, he felt unwanted and out of place everywhere he went, and he worked the graveyard shift at a casino, washing dishes. He had no love life and no prospects.

And then he met a cute girl named Paola on the Internet. She lived in Florida, but whatever, she was hot! Now he had a girlfriend he could brag about to his friends. After a while, she finally confessed that she wasn't "Paola" at all. She even revealed herself on a video chat, and she bore no resemblance to the girl in the pictures. But Ramon chose not to believe it! Instead, he demanded that she stop playing games with him—he insisted that *of course* she wasn't this new girl—and she went along with it, suddenly pretending that the girl in the video chat was her cousin and that it was just a test to see if Ramon really liked her.

So it went on. He bought her expensive gifts. He sent her money. He turned his head from the obvious truth. Why? Because his relationship with a "hot girl" gave him a sense of status for the first time in his life. The reality of what would happen should his relationship with Paola be revealed as a hoax seemed so much worse than just keeping up the charade. So he willingly participated in this cycle of dishonesty.

Even if they aren't as willfully blind as Ramon, most hopefuls turn their heads away from the truth at some point. I certainly did. But the question remains—how can catfish victims remain ignorant of the truth for so long? In some cases, these online relationships with fake people go on for years and years, with no video-chatting or real-life visits. I was on the hook for nine months. Looking back through my archive of emails, I can see how ridiculous some of my correspondence with Megan really was. But at the time, I was totally convinced. Why?

First of all, it *felt so good*. I *loved* talking to Megan. A lot of the other victims I've talked to say the same thing: that talking to their catfish was the best part of their day. They looked forward to getting home and chatting or emailing with them. Why would they question a good thing?

And then there is the issue of the emotional and time commitments. By the time I started to notice things that should have raised red flags, I was in too deep to really ask the hard questions. I'd spent too many hours on these relationships; I'd revealed too many of my feelings to Megan. I'd told her my secrets: about the tramp stamp tattoo I'd gotten at age seventeen (yep) and deeply regretted; about the insecurity that lay underneath my bravado. I'd even sent her some artful nudes my friend Michael Hart had taken of me. I felt like I'd been vulnerable with her, intimate in a way that I'd never been before.

This is quite common among the victims I've talked to. They say things along the lines of "I've been talking to this person for months/years. We've taken it slow. I opened up and revealed my emotions and deepest secrets. I'm so invested in this that I need to see it through." In other words, to walk away now would make all of that a waste.

Finally, it's time to throw out the word *addiction* again. People on *both* sides of these relationships get addicted to the correspondence. Because, like a drug, it makes them feel something. Because, like gambling, it's a risk, an unknown. There's a mysterious jackpot element: "Could this be my dream girl/guy?"

Addicted, emotionally dependent, and in too deep, the cat-fished hopefuls end up turning a blind eye. Part of the brain decides, "I don't want to know this is a lie, because then I'll not only have been betrayed but also have wasted all this time," and as a result, the hopeful *just doesn't see*.

————

Almost everybody feels undervalued in some way. As I've seen during my travels and correspondence with both catfish and hopefuls, lots of people feel unhappy with their lives—just as I did. But all it takes to lift your spirits is the affection and attention of one person.

Often, when I ask catfish victims to explain the connection that's kept them going for so long—what it is they *talk* about with the person on the other end of the line—they can't really point to anything specific. "She's just always there for me," they'll say. This amazes me. *What do you mean, "She's always there"?* I'll ask. *She's not there. She's online!* "Well, no, but she would always text me. You know, 'Good morning, How you doing?' " In other words, the most basic kind of communication.

It's a matter of just getting a text message from someone in the morning. An email that says "I'm thinking of you." A chat about what you ate for dinner. People go through their lives feeling so disappointed, unfulfilled, bored, and lonely that even the most rudimentary relationship—a positive and sup-portive regular correspondence—helps lift them. If you can show someone that you are thinking about them, if you go out of your way—even with just a text message—to say "Hey, I hope you are having a great day," the power of that is appar-ently overwhelming. So overwhelming that it blinds people to the fact that they are being hoaxed.

This is key; it reveals how little it takes for people to feel valued these days. We are so desperate for external validation that we'll even accept it from someone who may be lying to us. We want people to tell us that we are worthy, and our connections online are about confirming what we already want to believe about ourselves.

One catfish victim I'll always remember was a kid named Dorion (episode 205). He'd had a rough life—he was raised by a single mother, his house burned down, his mom had gotten sick, and he'd spent time being homeless. As he was going through all this, he met an (implausibly gorgeous) girl online. Despite the many red flags in her profile, he was so smitten with her that after two years of online correspondence, he was even considering dumping his terrific real-life girlfriend for this unconsummated virtual relationship. "She has been by my side through everything," he told me about his catfish. When he showed me their texts and emails and IMs, I was expecting there to be tear-jerking moments of intimacy and vulnerability. Instead, it was mostly your everyday correspondence, nothing that struck me as earth-shaking. But she had been a consistent presence during his darkest hours, and that was what he remembered. That consistency was so vital that it seemed to trump the girlfriend who'd known him only once his life was on the upswing.

This kid was smart enough to know that the photos his catfish sent him weren't really of her, but he didn't care, because she gave him affection and cared about him when he needed it the most.

And that, in a nutshell, is why people fall for catfish: They don't feel as if anyone else really cares about them. The catfish makes them feel special. They make them feel *loved*.

And isn't that the most compelling hook of all?

CHAPTER 5

How to Identify a Catfish

Never talk to strangers.

If you're anything like me, you probably heard this line from your mother about a million times while you were growing up. Well, sorry, Mom. Times have changed. We *all* talk to strangers now—all day, every day, everywhere we go online. It's just the nature of the world we live in.

So let's assume that—despite your mom—you are going to go out there and meet all kinds of strangers on the Internet. And, considering the number of fake social media profiles out there—like I said earlier, 83 million on Facebook alone—the odds are pretty good you'll run into a catfish at some point. How do you figure out if that fascinating stranger you're chatting with is actually who they say they are?

Believe it or not, I am not a clairvoyant catfish finder. I don't have access to supersecret government databases or mastermind software programs. And despite the fact that we've exposed several dozen catfish on my TV show, I'm not naturally adept at investigation. I had to learn my lessons the hard way.

In other words—everything that I do, you can do, too.

The good news is that most catfish can be identified with a skeptical eye, a little bit of common sense, and some basic Internet know-how. If you pay attention, you'll start to notice the little red flags that can prevent you from being hooked.

And so it's with a bit of hesitation that I now offer my advice on how to avoid being catfished. But I want to help, even if it means putting myself out of a job.

———

Here's a good rule of thumb to start with: If that person you've met online seems too good to be true—they probably are. I'm sorry to break it to you, but gorgeous, rich, successful, and busy world travelers typically don't have endless amounts of time to chat with strangers on the Internet.

If they have Abercrombie & Fitch abs? Red flag.

If they say they are a model? Big red flag.

Even someone who simply seems to like everything that you like should be taken with a grain of salt. Real people are more complex than that. Someone who seems to be your exact match in all things is probably tailoring the way they present themselves in order to appeal to you.

Through my years of observing catfish, I've learned that there are certain behavioral patterns that repeat themselves time and time again. For example: Catfish frequently disappear for days at a time, sometimes even weeks or months. They'll stop in the middle of an email conversation or Facebook chat and fail to reappear again for several days. They suddenly won't return phone calls or texts. What's probably happening is that they're having an internal struggle about what they're doing; they feel guilty about their lies, and they're worried about getting too close to you. Or they are cleverly manipulating you by being unavailable and mysterious in an effort to draw you in deeper.

If someone does this to you, and then returns with a vague or wild excuse for their absence, be very wary.

Similarly, catfish often seem to have terrible luck. Their lives are full of illness and catastrophe: car accidents, ER visits, family drama, even death. My Megan had a typical catfish profile, although I didn't recognize it at the time. In the eight months that I was in an online relationship with her, she was wrongfully arrested, got in several car accidents, had a brother get in trouble because of drugs, and nearly died while undergoing routine surgery. No one's life is that exciting all the time. No question, bad things do happen, but to that extent? Big warning sign. Especially if those dramatic events tend to coincide with plans to get together.

Catfish use this constant drama as a tool to both avoid conflict and draw on your sympathy: "Oh yeah, let's get together," they'll say. And then the day arrives and suddenly—"Oh no! My grandma is in the hospital! I'm so bummed out but I have to be with her." How can you be anything but sorry for them? Not only have they avoided getting together, but your empathy for their pain will draw you in even closer.

Catfish often pretend to be chronically ill, for the same reasons. (In fact, a widespread Internet scam consists of people pretending that they or their children have a terminal disease and then raising money from concerned online friends.) If someone you meet online tells you that they have cancer, ask them specific questions about their illness. If they're truly sick, they'll be able to tell you all about the doctors, medicine, and treatment. If they're not sick, they'll likely say something along the lines of "Oh, I don't want to talk about it." Of course, people who are terminally ill sometimes don't want to discuss their sickness, but if they have chosen to reach out to a stranger about their illness and then clam up when it comes to the details, it's suspicious. Use your logic and look for this kind of inconsistency.

Even if someone you've met online isn't exhibiting these behavior patterns, you still need to be careful. The first thing you should do when you meet *anyone* online, no matter how real they seem, is verify their existence. Are they really who they say they are? It may seem impossible to know, but honestly, the truth is not very hard to figure out. It's relatively painless, and it will save you a lot of agony in the long run.

When you meet someone online, Google them right off the bat. It may seem insane that I even have to tell people this, but I'm constantly shocked at just how many of our hopefuls on the show never bothered with this step. And don't just Google them and glance at the first few hits—go deep into the results. Make sure that what you dig up matches everything they've told you.

If you've watched the TV show *Catfish*, you already know that the next step is to hit up Google Images and search by image. Download any images your new friend has posted of himself and run them through this search engine. Check to see that the photos don't show up on someone else's Facebook page or website under a different name. Even if the person you're chatting with isn't lying about who they are, who knows what you might find: That photo might be posted on Sleazyguys.com by an ex-girlfriend who says that he's bailed out on child support. That's information you want to have.

Next, hit up Facebook.

Start by taking a good look at their Facebook friends. If they have an exceedingly high or exceedingly low number of friends, that's cause for concern. And are most of their friends either men or women, or is it appropriately mixed? Any girl that only has male friends on Facebook—or vice versa—should set off alarm bells.

Similarly, take measure of where most of their friends are from. Are these "friends" primarily people from around the world, or do they come from one area? Most *real* people are predominantly friends with people from their hometown, their college, and the places where they lived as adults. Of course, this isn't always the case, but if someone's friends hail from Africa and Australia and Japan, yet they have never left the United States, that's kind of weird. They probably don't know these people in real life. So what's the explanation?

Go through their photos on Facebook. If they only have photos of themselves, and no pictures with other people, that's definitely a red flag. (In fact, it's almost *worse* if they do end up being real, since it suggests that they are simply a self-obsessed egomaniac!)

Similarly, be skeptical if they have pictures of themselves with other people, but those other people aren't tagged. This applies to Facebook or Instagram. People tag their friends in photos. So if they're not tagging the people in their photos, it's probably because they don't actually know who those people are. Which means that *they* probably aren't who they say they are, either.

Look at what they've posted on their own Facebook page, and see what kinds of comments people are leaving on those posts. Are the people who are responding to them being specific? Do they sound like people who engage with this person face to face and attend real-world events with them? Or are their online correspondences just flattering banter from people who seem like strangers?

Martin $wagg

Amazing day. So excited for the beach this weekend.
Spent all day at the gym pumping up. Got my convertible ready!

 Tiffani Gorge! Dying!

 HOTTCHICA Crute

 J'anell OMGILYSM 🐱 🖤 🖤

 BigBootyBabe Have my babies!

If everything checks out so far and you're still interested in getting to know this person, it's time to dig deeper.

Reach out to some of their Facebook friends. Message those friends directly instead of commenting on a public post, and ask them how they know each other. Yes, it's awkward, but if that person really knows them, they'll be able to tell you how.

Ask them specific questions about their lives. It's incredible how often I meet people who haven't asked the most basic questions of the people they are supposedly in online relationships with. What does he do? "He makes music." How? "I don't know. I haven't asked him." Well, why not? Ask them about their family. Ask them about their job. Ask them about their friends. Get names, dates, places. Not only is it a way to get to know a person you like, it's also a good way to find out if they're really doing the things they say they do. If they *are*, they should have an easy time boring you with details. If they're not, they'll be suspiciously vague.

Take note of their profile username. Often, people use the same username on multiple social media sites—not just Facebook, Twitter, and Instagram, but also on discussion boards and in online communities. Look up the username and see what you can find.

Look up their phone number, if you have it. What name is it registered to? If nothing else, just look up the area code and make sure it's from the place where they say they live. Sometimes this means paying a small fee or even registering with a site, but that $19.99 could save you years of heartache and wasted time.

Online yearbooks are still fairly rare, but they do exist. It can't hurt to check out their high school and college websites to see if there's an online yearbook you can use to verify their name and face.

If they've told you where they work, call that business and ask for them. If they say they work at Staples, call Staples and ask to talk to Jesse in Printers and Fax Machines. Maybe the person will say, "Sure, hold on." Maybe they'll say, "No one named Jesse works here." Even if you hang up before they get on the line, at least you'll have confirmed their story.

Get their home address. Tell them you want to send them a letter, a postcard, something you made them: Where should you send it? If they hem and haw or give you a hard time, ask yourself—why?

Ask them if they've seen *Catfish*. Gauge their reaction.

Get photo proof: Give them a series of specific objects to wear or hold in a photograph. A carton of milk, a roll of toilet paper, and a toothbrush. There's no way they'll randomly find a picture of whoever they're pretending to be holding those three things.

And last—but definitely not least—*always* video verify. Put a video chat session at the very top of your agenda from the start. If they say they don't have a webcam—which, these days, is increasingly rare—ask them to do it at a friend's house. And if that's not possible either, ask them to text you a short video of themselves talking to you directly. Everyone has access to cameras these days; there's just no excuse anymore. If they like you, and they're real, they should do it.

So much of this advice is common sense, yet many of the people I encounter don't do any of the above. They don't want to come off as stalkers. They especially don't want the other person to find out what they are doing and think they are weird or creepy.

I get that. I'm not saying you should take all these actions every time you encounter someone new online, but be smart about how you interact with people you don't actually know. If you're attracted to someone, you've been talking to them for some time, and they still haven't video-chatted with you or met up in person, it's time to take some steps to protect yourself. (See chapter 13 for safe ways to meet in person.)

Sure, it's awkward to sneak around someone's back asking questions. But how much more awkward will it be when you find out that your French supermodel girlfriend is actually a teenage boy from Kansas City?

CHAPTER 6

Catfish: The TV Show

Not long after the documentary *Catfish* was released, I began to get emails. Tons of emails. It was like the floodgates had opened, and everyone who had ever been involved in a fake online relationship was contacting me. They were relieved to finally have someone to share their experiences with. And it wasn't just people who had been catfished. I was suddenly the go-to guy for anyone who had gone through an experience online that left them feeling vulnerable, or unhappy, or concerned that they were being "had." Overnight I became an expert on all kinds of frustrating and enigmatic online relationships, a guru on digital love, as it were.

In a way, it was the perfect answer to all the frustrations that had led to me being a victim of catfishing in the first place. I'd gotten involved with my catfish as a result of my desire to be a better person, my longing to be useful and appreciated. Well, now I could really *be* that Nev.

Miraculously, I'd been the victim of a hoax and had handled it with sensitivity and compassion, had demonstrated an ability to listen to my catfish and to forgive her despite all the mistakes she'd made. I'd finally been the nonjudgmental, sensitive, caring, *nice* guy I'd always wanted to be, and it had—fortuitously—ended up on tape for the whole world to see. The whole world thought I *was* that guy. Which meant I had the rare opportunity to make Nice Nev the New Nev—permanently.

As these stories poured into my inbox—as strangers stopped me in the street to tell me about their experiences—I was both shocked and amazed. Clearly I'd tapped into a previously undiscussed issue that was plaguing our society. My experience was just the tip of the iceberg: There was a huge underground river of relationships taking place that were just like mine. And what surprised me the most was how many different types of people—of different ages, backgrounds, vocations—were experiencing the same thing. I was getting letters from teenagers and from senior citizens, from rich people and poor people, from all over the earth.

Finally, I turned to my brother, Rel, and said, "This is crazy. We should follow up on these stories and make a show about them." And so *Catfish: The TV Show* was born.

———

Catfish: The TV Show has been on the air for three seasons now. People come up to me all the time and want to know what goes on behind the scenes. For those of you who are curious, here's a (very) brief FAQ.

Question 1: "Hey, Nev, how exactly does the show get made? Who contacts who?"

First, people write in to our show, asking to be featured on an episode. It can be the hopeful or—more rarely—the catfish, who wants to confess. Whether they write in for help meeting the person they are falling in love with or are looking for the perfect opportunity to finally come clean, people come to the show with the same hope of finally having a physical interaction with the person they've been digitally pursuing.

We start by spending two full days with our hopeful—getting to know them, seeing where they live, often meeting friends or family, and also investigating this person they are in love with. It's interesting to note that when we come to help these people, they really have to put their lives on hold—take time off from their job, miss their classes. We arrive in their lives like a tornado and bring everything to a stop while we lift them up into the air and spin them around for a week. In a good way, of course. A gentle, loving tornado.

Then we travel with them to the hometown of their potential online love, and by our fourth day together, we are going to meet the catfish. Sometimes it goes well, sometimes it doesn't. On the fifth day we reconvene with the two of them and spend some private time with the catfish to help them open up and understand why they were doing what they were doing. And then, poof! We are gone.

The five or six days that we are there are arguably the most exciting, confusing, emotional, and difficult days of that person's life. During that time, a relationship in which they were incredibly invested either grows significantly or crashes and burns. We have to be *in it* with them. Max and I completely invest ourselves, engage with these people, and do everything we can to support, encourage, inform, and advise. We do our best to create a relaxed and comfortable environment so that people will open up to us.

To be completely honest, doing this show can be emotionally exhausting for us, as well. I often don't know how I feel about the lying catfish I just met, or even about the hopeful who has been engaged in this relationship for so long despite some incredibly obvious red flags. I often have no idea what to say to the people I am trying to help. I can't offer them an easy fix. And sometimes I feel like no matter what I say, I'm not going to get through to them. Anyway, who am I to help them, when I myself am often just as confused and uncertain about life?

At this point, I try to have a long conversation with Max or our awesome showrunner, Dave Metzler. They remind me that our purpose isn't to solve the problems of the people we meet. Instead, it's to listen and to give these people an opportunity to think about how they feel and what's driving their actions—sometimes for the first time in their lives.

Question 2: "Okay, Nev. But don't the people who contact you know that the show is usually about fake relationships? That it's almost always a hoax?"

Sure. But the truth is that I'm their last resort. They believe that the show is the best chance they have for finally meeting the person they are in love with and getting some answers. It's not news to them that they may be catfished. That's why they've reached out to me in the first place. Somewhere in the back of their mind, they know that this relationship they're having isn't quite right. And they are ready to learn the truth, for better or for worse.

But they also think they are going to be the exception to the rule—because exceptions do happen! They are holding out hope, clearly. What I love about our show is that we try to inform our hopefuls of what we've discovered prior to introducing them to their catfish face to face. It'd be so much more entertaining to not tell them anything we find, and watch the train wreck as they knock on the door—but we try to warn them, gently. We may be a reality show, but we try to be kinder and gentler than real life will ever be.

Sometimes, though, I still have to remind myself that this is someone's *reality*. I remember sitting in a car with Lauren (episode 204) on the way to meet her supposed catfish, Derek. Lauren was playing her cards close to the vest, so I kept pressuring her to think about the worst possible outcome in an effort to elicit some kind of emotional reaction. "What's wrong with this guy?" Max and I kept asking her. "Maybe he's hiding something? It's been eight years!" "Let's keep our guard up." We didn't want her to be blindsided.

Finally, to her credit, Lauren stopped us. "You're making me feel like shit before I meet him," she said. "You guys, it's not always bullshit. You do this all the time for people. But for me, it's new. I don't do this."

"This is not a show for you," I said, realizing. "This is your *life*."

"Yeah," she said, crying.

It was a really great wake-up call for both me and Max. We may always try to be nice and empathetic guys, but you can never really understand what someone else is feeling. Does the victim suspect their "love" is a hoax? Maybe, but emotions aren't that black-and-white. After Lauren called us out, we tried hard not to repeat the same mistake. We remind ourselves constantly that the feelings of a human being are far more important than our television show.

Question 3: "Don't you ever think, 'God, these people are stupid'? How do you maintain such a nonjudgmental attitude?"

Well, I'm heavily sedated through most of it. Just kidding.

The honest answer is that it *is* hard. Just like the people watching the TV show, I often want to roll my eyes when I hear outlandish stories of digital romance. But right before I succumb to the instinct to laugh or be dismissive, I remind myself that I had the exact same thing happen to me. Anybody who heard my story would have said the same thing: "How can you be so dumb? You don't actually believe that, do you? An eight-year-old selling her paintings for thousands of dollars?" But I believed all of it.

To the hopefuls having these relationships, it feels very real. There's a backlog of phone calls, text messages, and emails that we don't have time to show on air—if the hopeful even managed to save them all. We don't have the advantage of showing our viewers the slow, piece-by-piece trickle of how each relationship developed. When you talk to someone every day, you feel like they care about you, and they do! But when you fast-forward and sum up an entire digital relationship from the outside, it often looks totally implausible. Which is why I'm equipped for this job: I know how it feels to be in that kind of relationship on a daily basis.

So even if, in the back of my mind, I'm thinking, "This is so obvious; how can they not see this?" I remind myself that (1) *I* didn't see it; and (2) there's always a chance it's real. We've seen it on our show. The world is crazy; weird stuff happens every day. So I'm not going to make any assumptions.

Question 4: "Max! We want more Max! Tell us all about Max!"

I've known Max since high school. He and Rel met at a UCLA summer film workshop: Rel was walking down the hall, singing "The Confrontation" from *Les Misérables*—"*Valjean, at last, we see each other plain*"—when, directly behind him, he heard some guy singing the next line of the song—"*Monsieur, le Mayor, you wear a different chain*." It was Max. The rest was history. Max became my friend by default; I spent my high school years tagging along after him and my brother.

Max wasn't originally supposed to be on *Catfish* at all (I know; crazy, right?)—I had a different friend picked out to be my on-camera partner. Max stepped in to temporarily pinch-hit when my friend had a scheduling conflict, and after we saw Max on the screen, we all knew he was perfect. The yin to my yang. It's turned into an amazing three-year partnership. But he still holds that fact over my head: "I wasn't even your first choice!"

I've learned a lot from Max—especially how to be more self-aware and considerate to the people in my life. I marvel at his filmmaking abilities. He's taught me so much about storytelling. I feel lucky to call him one of my best friends.

We've had a few fights; for example, during season 2, we

were the only people sleeping at a bed-and-breakfast in Burlington, Iowa—even the owner wasn't staying there. I'd gone out for dinner with the crew, leaving Max at the hotel, and I decided to sneak back in and make haunted house sounds to mess with him. He got a little spooked—though he won't admit it—and then a lot annoyed, as I kept the sounds going far too long. When I finally revealed myself, he lunged at me, and we ended up wrestling in the living room. It ended when we realized that his nose was bleeding, and I ran to get tissues. We didn't want to hurt each other; it was just a best friends' tussle.

Question 5: "What's it like for you and Max, being on the road together so much?"

Max and I are total opposites in the way we travel.

Max can't wake up in the morning. He's a night owl—editing all night—and wants to sleep in. He sleeps with the shades totally closed: He's a cave dweller. You literally have to pull the sheets off him and jump on the bed to get his day started.

I couldn't be more different: I'm a bright, chipper morning person. I jump out of bed and am immediately energized. But once we are both up, Max puts on music—usually EDM (electronic dance music)—and we end up having a morning dance party.

Max gets to the hotel and it's as if his suitcase is spring-loaded. He opens the lid and everything erupts. His girlfriend, Priscilla, is a stylist and fashion blogger who takes him shopping and puts his outfits together. I give him a really hard time about that, probably because I secretly wish that I had my own personal stylist, too.

Meanwhile, I am always knolling. If you don't know what that word means, it's the process of keeping things neat, everything at right angles. (You can watch a hilarious Tom Sachs / Van Neistat film about knolling online.[1]) I'm constantly making sure that things are squared up and symmetrical. My hotel room always looks like the cleaning lady *just* left.

Max and I shared rooms in season 1 and—despite our differences—it was great. But these days, we get our own rooms. It's probably better for everyone.

Question 6: "Do you guys have a lot of material you don't use? What doesn't make it on the show?"

For every episode of *Catfish*, we have exactly forty-two minutes to tell the story of the online relationship we're investigating. In order to get those forty-two minutes, we spend five or six entire days with our subjects, eight to ten hours a day. Do the math: That's a whole lot of time we spend with these people that ends up on the editing room floor.

It's incredibly frustrating to me that so many of the storylines from these people's lives just won't make it into the final episode. Life is complicated. We work hard to draw all this information out of our subjects—their motives and all the nuanced details that explain why this person feels so strongly about that person even though they've never met. It often gets distilled into a three-second graphic of a text message that says "I love you so much, baby." That's not sufficient to illustrate a six-month—let alone a six-year—love affair.

Question 7: "Does being on the show ever change the lives of the people you've met?"

In most cases, the people we've met on the show have not spent a lot of time thinking about—much less talking about—how they really feel. No one has ever *asked* them, so they haven't pushed themselves to figure it out. Personally, I've been in therapy since I was a teenager (you've read enough of this book to understand why), and my expectations for personal insight are high. But that's not fair. Often, we think we know how the catfish and hopeful feel, and we're wrong. I have to remind myself, "I don't know how this person is feeling. I'm just here to encourage them to think about their feelings so they can make sense of their actions."

Sometimes the people on our show really do get insight into their behavior and motivations. So for those who are willing to do some soul-searching, I think the show does change their lives. But it always breaks my heart when I follow up with a catfish and ask them what they've learned and they say, "Don't get into Internet relationships." Because that's not the point of our show.

What *do* I want those people to have learned?

- Know what you want!
- Be comfortable with who you are!
- Demand respect!
- Treat others kindly!

The emotional issues that catfish face aren't so different from yours and mine. It's just that their behavior is more extreme. Through the people I've met while making the show, I've come to understand that catfishing reveals what's missing in *all* of our lives: true communication and self-awareness. The lessons that catfish and their hopefuls need to learn are the same ones that we all should learn.

Including myself. It's taken me thirty years—with a lot of help along the way—to understand how I should be living my life, why I should appreciate myself, and how to challenge myself. It may not be possible to transfer that hard-earned wisdom within the confines of a TV show, but my hope is that through the documentary, the TV show, and now through this book, I have at the very least begun a cultural conversation about how we are relating to one another and to ourselves.

PART TWO

How to Live and Love Online

Catfish are the symptom, not the cause, of one of the biggest challenges we face today: how to conduct ourselves in a world in which our friendships, love affairs, and day-to-day interactions frequently take place online.

More than ever, people are choosing to invest more in their digital lives than in their everyday experiences. An entire generation has shifted to feeling more satisfied by posting a photo on Instagram or receiving a hundred "likes" on a Facebook comment than by going to a party and interacting in person with their peers. It's become easier to maintain an online relationship than to make a real connection.

And yet social media encourages half-truths and downright lies, which undermine the bases of all those relationships. This is why it's important for everyone—not just catfish—to start living honest online lives. If we're going to live and love on social media, we need new guidelines to help us present our digital selves authentically, communicate wisely, and date effectively—not to mention how to protect ourselves against bullies, trolls, haters, and, yes, catfish.

Consider this section a prototype of the Golden Rules for Social Media, guidelines that I hope will help everyone lead a safer, more truthful, and more productive online existence.

CHAPTER 7

My Catfish Story, Part Two

Megan was gorgeous. No question about it. I spent hours combing through her Facebook photos, posting comments about how beautiful I thought she was. She told me how handsome I was, how much she wanted to meet me. Our emails to each other grew frank and flirty.

Hey Nev-

I have a confession to make. The only reason I went back on Facebook was to try to get to know you a little better.

———

Hey Megan-

. . . the feeling is mutual. No need for apologies at all.

We began to Facebook message each other almost daily. Soon, a pastel sketch arrived in the mail, stuck inside the latest package of Abby originals. It was a picture of me, a sketch that Megan had drawn based off my Facebook profile picture.

I think my favorite photo of you is the one that I drew you from. It's so quiet and peaceful. When I see it, it makes me think of falling asleep on your chest with your hands laced through my hair. I think I should stop thinking now, I wish I could.

Sweet dreams-
Megan

By mid-April, I'd sent her my phone number. The woman who called me was breathy and soft-spoken. Her voice was high and full of shy laughter, and although our conversation was hesitant at first, we quickly grew comfortable with each other.

Hey Nev-

It was so nice talking with you last night. You're so easy to talk to and I love the sound of your voice. You're quite charming with your wit and humor.

I hope to talk to you again soon. I was so nervous about talking with you that I forgot most everything I wanted to ask you and now I want to know so much more about you.

After we said our good byes I went and took my bath and fell asleep in the tub. Abby woke me up at 3:45 and asked "Why were you talking to Nev on the phone?" . . . I have to stay one step ahead of that girl.

I have to get back to work.

I hope you're having a beautiful day!

Peace-
Megan

Within the week, we had each other on speed dial.

At first, I attempted to keep some kind of reality check on the situation. After all, Megan lived in Michigan, she was younger than me—and, oh yeah, I had a girlfriend in New York City. My emails to Megan often vacillated between brazen flirtation and cool standoffishness, sexy talk and hard truth.

Hey Nev-

I'm not trying to make you uncomfortable, I'm just being honest so please forgive me. Trust me, this is just as awkward for me as it is for you. I've been overwhelmingly attracted to you for sometime now. I'm not sure how or why that happened because honestly it just doesn't happen to me. So many things I see in you are qualities that I find attractive and I was hoping for something to happen between us. I think about you constantly. When I close my eyes I dream of being with you, going places, doing things together and so much more that I don't want to say for fear of really making you feel uncomfortable.

Peace - Meg

————

OK, Megan

I have to admit that through our getting to know each other over the past months, I have found myself thinking about you a lot also. There is a natural attraction between us that would be silly to ignore. The only reason I told you to cool down with the compliments was because it is just a little strange to have someone tell me that I have such a nice voice and how handsome I am. I would have told my mom to stop telling me that too, it wasn't my way of trying to give you a clue... it just feels funny to hear it.

That being said, I do think it's important for us to remember that our whole relationship is based on the mystery and improbability of it ever becoming something. At this point, it's clear that our lives will overlap in some way and I'm really happy about that. I just have no idea what our collective future will hold and don't want to go forward with any expectations.

Ok. I'm going to stop before I lose my focus.

Let me know what you think.

- Nev

Despite my attempts to keep Megan at arm's length, the truth was that we were talking every few days, and frequently discussing our attraction to each other. I was still officially with my girlfriend, Katie, but I wasn't exactly letting that get in the way of my flirtation with Megan. (Go ahead, call me a sleaze—you wouldn't be wrong.) I figured that I wasn't cheating on Katie just by emailing and talking to another girl. Megan lived halfway across the country! We weren't even having phone sex. (Well, not yet.)

But the truth was, a dangerously real-feeling relationship was developing. Even though I insisted to Megan—and everyone else—that we were "just friends," it was clearly a lot more complicated than that. So perhaps it was no surprise when, not long after the correspondence with Megan began to heat up, Katie and I broke up.

My and Megan's lives grew more and more entangled. Although my focus was increasingly on Megan, I was still heavily engaged with the entire family in Ishpeming. Abby's paintings based on my work were selling like hotcakes—well enough that the family could afford to buy an old run-down JCPenney in town and turn it into a gallery—and thanks to our business agreement I soon got my first check in the mail, for five hundred dollars.

Sometimes it felt like this fun, kooky Michigan family

was a sitcom, and I was the sole audience member. I had an exclusive front row seat to this exciting and weird show. Bored with my New York life, I latched on. Soon, I was emailing and instant-messaging not just with Megan, Angela, and Abby, but with Megan's extended family and friends. And they, in turn, were chatting online with *my* friends: my mom and Angela talked on the phone; my brother Facebooked with several of the Ishpeming crew; another friend of mine was constantly on IM and email with pretty much everyone up in Michigan.

Megan was my magical unicorn girl. She seemed to have it all: She was young, beautiful, active, flirtatious, and sexy. Her interests mirrored mine: She was a ballet dancer, an artist, a musician. She had focus: She was even a homeowner, buying a small horse farm before she'd hit twenty. She was a bad-ass who scuba dived and talked about going to work on a fishing boat in Alaska for the summer with her father. But she was also appealingly fragile and vulnerable—her family constantly told me to be sensitive about her low self-esteem. To top it all off (and perhaps this was where I should have gotten skeptical), she was a virgin.

I liked who *I* was with her, too. Usually I'd jump right into bed with the girls I met. This was the first time I'd been forced to take it slow. It felt like we were on a perpetual first date. And it's easy, on a first date, to curate how you present yourself, showing off only your most desirable qualities. I played up my kindness and generosity.

Another thing about first dates: They are full of potential. As Max says, mystery is the greatest aphrodisiac. Sure, I had plenty of girls I could pursue in New York, but this woman's lack of availability made her intriguing and exciting. *Imagining* sleeping with her was way more interesting than actually getting laid. The potential in this perfect virgin halfway across the country was way more alluring than the reality of being intimate with a complicated real human being in New York.

And wow, was there a lot of sexual titillation to keep me imagining it. At the end of May, Tim Hobbins—who, besides being Abby's art dealer, was a professional photographer—sent me a pile of photographs for which Megan had posed. They were highly sexy art photos: Megan naked, her back arched. Megan topless, with her hair coyly covering her breasts. Megan in sexy lingerie. Megan and Angela, naked, laughing. Megan in body paint. Megan in a fuzzy hat and jeans and nothing in between.

The pictures were stunning—and featured heavily in my nocturnal fantasy life (I'm sure you know what I mean). And in return, I sent her my own sexy art photographs—of myself naked, holding a stuffed deer head in strategic positions.

Hey Handsome-

I've been thinking about you all day. I kept wondering what it would be like to have you here with me. I would love to take the boat out just you and me. We could do some shallow dives where we wouldn't have to get all geared up, we could just free dive or snorkel. You'd be amazed at what you can see when you dive the shipwrecks here. They are hauntingly beautiful.

I'd love to set anchor far out from shore and lay on deck in the sun with you. Of course we'd have to put sunscreen on each other. I'd love to run my hands over your back and chest feeling your skin under my finger tips. I love your chest! I want to nuzzle into it while you lace your fingers through my hair. I also love when you have a little scruff of a beard. It makes me want to touch your face and kiss you. I would love to stay out on the water for hours just kissing you, touching you, exploring your body with my kisses. It makes my mouth water thinking of what could happen if you would let me have you.

I don't understand how I can feel so strongly for you when we are so different in so many ways. Your friendship means the world to me but I can't seem to keep myself from thinking that there might be something more between us. I keep trying to remind myself of the things you've already written to me about us not being able to be together because of the different stages we are at in our lives and how we can only be friends at this point but I can't seem to stop myself from wanting you in a more intimate way. I'm so anxious to come meet you!

Peace-
Megan

Not long after that, I Photoshopped myself into one of the half-naked pictures she'd sent me. We agreed that we looked great together.

Inevitably, it escalated into sexts:

Megan: I'm at home baking pies.

Me: Save a pie for me.

(Later)

Megan: I'm in the bathtub, thinking of you.

Me: Funny, I was thinking about you in the shower earlier.

Megan: Mmmm. I'd like to think about that. You know, I'll always have a pie for you, babe.

Me: Cherry?

Megan: Cherry. My body is craving your touch tonight.

Me: What exactly would you do if I had you there?

Megan: I'd have you in the tub between my legs...

I'll spare you the rest—and myself the embarrassment—but you get the idea. It was intimate. It was exciting. I'd never had an exchange like that.

As time passed, I began to think more and more seriously about going to stay with Megan, to see if she was everything I thought she was. Maybe I would even move up to Michigan. Try to be in a relationship with this girl. Life in New York wasn't *all that*, so why not uproot myself and start over in a whole new town with a whole new life? It felt like a really appealing option—and, although I didn't admit this to myself, an easy escape, a cheap solution to my chronic dissatisfaction.

In the meantime, Megan talked frequently about coming to visit me in New York. We made plans a half dozen times. But something always seemed to get in the way. (If I were investigating this relationship on *Catfish*, this is where I would raise a skeptical eyebrow.)

- In April, a family trip was planned to New York—Megan, Abby, and their stepbrother Alex planned to drive out—but it was aborted before it was even under way:

Hey Nev-

... I'm not going to be able to come to New York this coming weekend and unfortunately it doesn't look like Abby will be allowed to either.

My truck died last weekend and I missed an entire weekend of work. No work=no pay :(

To try to catch up financially I agreed to work Friday thru Monday this upcoming weekend.

- In May, Abby, Megan, and Megan's friend Josh tried a second time to organize a weekend visit to New York. My mother even corresponded with Angela about having Abby stay at her apartment. We bought ballet tickets in anticipation. They decided to drive out to save money. But not long after they got on the road to New York, I began to get texts from Megan. Abby was sick; they'd pulled over to let her throw up. Then the van had broken down. They were stranded in a small town two states away. Instead of forging on, they turned around and went back home. I was disappointed, but I wasn't upset—how could I be? They had it worse than I did.

- In June, a few days before she was supposed to come visit me, Megan went to the doctor to fix a deviated septum, a lingering problem from an old horse riding accident. When they sedated her, she had a reaction to the anesthesia, and she flatlined. The doctors revived her, but of course, the trip was canceled. And when I offered to visit her in the hospital instead, she refused—she didn't want me to meet her like that; besides, things with her family were too crazy.

- In July, Abby and Megan planned to come visit. But then Abby's father insisted that she fly out to San Jose to visit him instead. Megan decided to make the drive by herself, but fell asleep at the wheel in the middle of the night and crashed on a deserted road. She walked for two hours before she was picked up by the police, who arrested her on suspicion of a DUI. Instead of spending the weekend with me, she spent it in jail.

This girl seemed to have the worst luck *ever*. And yet I didn't question her stories.

Looking back, there are also countless emails and recalled phone conversations that, knowing what I know now, make it clear that I was talking to a catfish. There seemed to be no limit to her incredible stories—not just the near-constant drama and car mishaps, but also the father who was a commercial fisherman in Alaska, the former home that had burned down, the time that Alex and his friends were caught selling drugs (a story that Angela confirmed by sending me a news article about the drug arrest of some unnamed local teens). Or the fact that a nineteen-year-old student could buy a $225,000 horse farm on a part-time vet assistant's salary. Or that an eight-year-old girl could sell so many paintings that her family could open an art gallery.

But instead of setting off alarm bells, the stories just drew me in further and made me more sympathetic to the family's fascinating, problem-plagued life.

And no, we never video-chatted. Call me naive. But I didn't have a webcam, and neither did Megan. (This was 2008, before webcams were standard in phones and laptops.) Anyway, it never crossed my mind that I needed to video verify her. I'd seen a million pictures of her, and the photos had people in them who were active on their own Facebook profiles. People whom I was communicating with, too. How much more *real* did I need?

And yes, I had Googled Megan, and found nothing. But since she'd been telling me about her dislike and avoidance of the Internet since the first day I'd met her, that didn't surprise me.

Abby, on the other hand, occasionally nagged at me. Why weren't there any online articles about this young prodigy's artwork? I thought that was weird, but then again, it didn't prove or disprove anything. Besides, I was getting checks in the mail from her art sales. It was a dead end, so I didn't think much of it.

Some of my friends were skeptical—including Katie, my now-ex-girlfriend, and my brother, who by this point was filming my life incessantly, as he found the entire relationship to be incredibly entertaining and unusual. But for every question, I had a perfectly good explanation. And because I seemed so convinced, I was able to convince everyone around me. Which only convinced me even further: The more people believed my story, the more I believed it. I dug myself in deeper and deeper.

It turns out it's a lot easier to disprove the truth than it is to prove a lie.

————

Over the months of our friendship, Angela, Megan, and Alex had sent me music that their family had recorded together. Most of it was what you'd expect from a small garage band—as in, not gonna blow your socks off. But there were a few songs that stuck with me, including a pretty song called "Downhill," with Angela singing and Megan playing guitar. I was impressed and put it in heavy rotation on our office stereo.

The last week of July, Rel, Henry, and I headed to Vail, Colorado, for a two-week job making dance documentaries. I'd spoken to Megan about flying her out to visit during the trip, but we hadn't yet figured out the logistics. Not long after we arrived in Vail, during an evening messaging session, Megan mentioned that she and Alex were noodling around recording music. Was there any particular song that I wanted to hear?

Megan: I take requests
  but piano you'll have to wait until tomorrow for
  I don't have one at my house
Me: tennessee stud!!!
  please please please do tennessee stud for me
  real sexy
Megan: I think I can handle that
Me: ok, you have 15 minutes
Megan: lol

An hour later, an MP3 landed in my inbox. The recording was crappy, but the song was gorgeous: A throaty, husky woman's voice accompanied by an acoustic guitar. Rel, Henry, and I were all blown away. "I can't believe she just did that!" I bragged, and then, eager to show off the talents of the rest of Megan's family, I told Rel and Henry about Angela's rendition of "Downhill." One thing led to another—we wanted to find the lyrics to "Downhill," so we punched some of the words from the song into Google, looking for the original version… and moments later came across a YouTube video of a musician named Amy Kuney, singing a song called "All Downhill from Here."

It was the *exact* same song.

We listened to the recording again, stunned. It was unmistakably the same version of the song that Angela claimed to have sung herself. There was no question about it: Angela had lied. They had *all* lied, including Megan.

Curious, we next plugged "Tennessee Stud" into YouTube, and sure enough, there it was, on the fourth page of search results: an amateur recording of a girl singing "Tennessee Stud" at a bar in New York. By now, it was clear what was going on: Angela, Megan, and Alex were downloading live recordings from YouTube and trying to pass them off as their own.

I didn't know what to think. Why would they lie to me about their music? They were so great; why did they feel the need to pretend to me that they were serious musicians if they weren't? I was angry enough to fire off messages to Angela, Megan, and Alex, telling them what I'd discovered and demanding an explanation. Instead of apologizing or admitting to their deception, they grew defensive. Alex claimed that they'd used the "Tennessee Stud" bar song as a model for their own recording, and that he'd simply accidentally sent me the wrong file; the original, rather than their cover.

As for "Downhill," they all claimed that it wasn't identical to the Amy Kuney song—it just *sounded* a lot like it because that was what they were trying to achieve.

Me: so?
   do you have an explanation for why the songs sound so similar?

Megan: It's a cover song
   they're suppose to sound similar

Me: maybe you should call me…cause im about to be very upset

Megan: I'm already very upset

Me: well me too
   i can't believe you are lying to me
   wow
   im so shocked

Megan: WHAT!
   Are you kidding me?

Me: right back at ya
   we need to speak now please
   im sure we can figure this out

Megan: It sounds like you have already made up your mind that
I'm a liar

Me: no, but i would love to hear from you that its not true
i want to believe you
really

By now, I was pissed off and growing more suspicious by the minute. It was obvious they were lying; I thought it was ridiculous that they were spinning it to make me the aggressor. And I was also confused and hurt. I'd opened up to Megan, had become emotionally invested in our relationship. If the music was a lie, what else had she been lying about?

Rel and Henry were already on the case, proving their skills as amateur private investigators on Google. By the next day, we'd made a series of alarming discoveries. That horse farm Megan had told me she'd bought, the one where I'd sent her postcards? It was still listed as for sale. So was the JCPenney building in downtown Ishpeming that Abby had said she was renovating for a gallery. Maybe the listings just hadn't been updated, but in light of the lies about the music, that didn't seem so likely.

It was growing clear that Megan and her family had spun a web of lies for me. Why? The only explanation I could come up with was that maybe they were intimidated by my New York lifestyle and wanted to appear more cosmopolitan and accomplished than they really were. Maybe they were poor and wanted to appear rich (but in that case, why were they sending me money?). Maybe they just felt a need to impress.

The one thing that I never questioned was their existence. Not even when Rel, Henry, and I decided to spontaneously fly from Vail to Michigan and go confront them, face to face.

CHAPTER 8

A Brave New World Wide Web

Back when I was a teenager, in the late 1990s, there was no Facebook. (Yeah, I'm *that* old.) If I liked a girl, I didn't "poke" her. I didn't follow her on Twitter or post on her wall. I wrote a note—on *actual paper*—and passed it to her in class. Or I picked up a telephone and called her—on a landline, *at her house*, awkwardly having to ask her mom if she was home and available, since hardly anyone had cell phones. If I had something I wanted to say to her, I had to do it in person. If I wanted to learn more about her, I had to actually spend time with her.

Fortunately, I was born with the gift of confidence (or maybe I just didn't have the capacity to be embarrassed). I was fearless when it came to connecting with girls, whether it was writing notes as a kid or buying drinks as an adult.

It's a good thing that I *was* confident, because in those days, it was also a lot harder to meet new people. You didn't have access to a massive online network where you could contact hundreds of people who were loosely connected to you through some mysterious algorithm. Instead, your dating pool was limited to the people in your school or your after-school clubs and the kids you met on vacations. I remember going to "socials" at my summer camp, sharing one clammy-handed dance with a girl from our sister camp, and spending the rest of the summer sending letters across the lake to her. Not exactly modern romance.

By the time I arrived at Sarah Lawrence, in 2002, Myspace was big. I wasn't a fan; I had a page but I hardly ever checked it, and I didn't really get the hype. But by my junior year, Facebook had launched, and suddenly I was hooked. Being on Facebook felt like an obligation: It was the cool thing to do. In almost no time at all, if you weren't on Facebook, you didn't exist.

That marked the beginning of a seismic shift in the way people across the globe interact with one another. Thanks to the rise of social media and digital technology, everything about how we communicate has changed. The United States Postal Service is going bankrupt, while the average teenager sends 3,339 texts per month.[2] And if Facebook—nonexistent a decade ago—were a country, it would be the world's third-largest, containing one of every nine people on the planet.[3] We even date digitally now: A quarter of all "millennials" date online, often through increasingly enormous dating sites like Match.com but also just by meeting other people on the Internet.[4] As an alternative to dances, parties, or bars, social media sites are where we go to meet one another.

Everything now is about social media: There's Twitter (200 million users and counting); online gaming communities like Call of Duty and World of Warcraft; photo-sharing sites like Instagram and Pinterest; blogs and Tumblrs and Snapchat and Chatroulette and vlogs and Vines and whatever else will be out there by the time this book rolls off the press. Every day, it seems, there's a new social media platform, a new way for people to meet each other digitally. There are so many ways to be friends online that the idea of just going to grab a coffee with someone feels downright *archaic*.

Why do we like these social media platforms so much more

than the old system of telephones and paper and meeting in person?

People say that social media has opened up a world of information, and has helped us connect to share ideas. That's absolutely true. But books and stories have been doing that for centuries. And yes, the Internet made it easier to meet people! But why do we really love our social media? It's because online we don't have to deal with the awkwardness of real-time interactions and rejections; we feel safer behind the screen.

And yet this shift to a nonphysical way of interacting has created a whole new series of problems. Sure, the Internet has opened up an exciting spectrum of communication. It's changed the world in positive ways, allowed creativity to flourish, started revolutions, enabled new and profound connections. It can be an amazing tool when used correctly. But it's also taken us away from doing what, in my humble opinion, humans are meant to do: living our lives where we are, using our bodies and not just our minds.

———

There's a great short film from 2013 called *Noah* that captures the disconnectedness of a life lived completely online. It takes place entirely on the computer screen of a kid named Noah as he obsessively clicks from Facebook to porn to online games to Chatroulette and back to Facebook. His girlfriend, Amy, Skypes him, says something cryptic about the status of their relationship, and then hangs up. Rather than picking up the phone and talking to Amy about what's going on, Noah obsesses over her status updates, hacks into her private Facebook messages, becomes convinced that she's cheating on him, and ultimately gets dumped via online chat.

The movie ends with a lonely Noah desperately seeking some kind of interaction with a human, begging a total stranger on Chatroulette to talk to him.[5]

If you ask me, this film—much like *Her*, the terrific Spike Jonze film about a guy who falls in love with his computer's operating system—sums up what's going wrong in the Facebook era. We may think we are being more social thanks to the Internet—like Noah, we'll spend the entire day chatting simultaneously with friends, romantic partners, and total strangers—but in fact, we are being *less* social, since our communication doesn't involve any physical interaction at all. Sure, we're communicating more, but those interactions are not as meaningful or intimate.

> "Oh, great! I don't have to actually call my mom and talk to her on the phone anymore. I'll just email her!"

> "I have to break up with my girlfriend? Awkward! I'll just text her."

> "My friend's dad died and I don't know what to say, so I'll just post something on his wall. It's so much easier!"

And it is! It's *so much easier*. That's why the Internet is so successful: It took something difficult—human communication—and made it easy. It took away the vulnerability.

When we're far away from our friends and loved ones, these tools can be helpful and relationship-maintaining. But when we resort to them out of laziness or fear, we are eroding our relationships, not building them.

Don't get me wrong; I'm as guilty of this as anyone. I've gone weeks where I've talked with my dad only via text.

DON'T USE YOUR

TO COMMUNICATE.

USE YOUR

VOICE

Because talking to my dad—or mom, or grandmother, or friend—in person means *caring*. If I can hear his voice and he can hear mine, or if we are sitting face to face, emotions are involved. I have to show genuine interest, and if he says something that's difficult for me to hear, I'm confronted with a situation I can't avoid. And if I get up and walk away, it's rude or hurtful or embarrassing.

In person, it's hard to hide how we feel; we can't escape seeing the judgment in the expressions of the person sitting across from us, the way we can online. Then there are the heavy, awkward conversational silences, and the fact that we can't avoid responsibility for the impact our words have on the person sitting across from us.

In other words, when we are face to face, we can't ignore the emotions involved. It's riskier. But with social media and technology, there's a way to interact without any of that challenging emotional stuff. We have, over the past decade, turned to a form of communication that is devoid of all those things that make human interaction exciting. It's a safe way to communicate, but it's sterile and leaves no room for the thrill of a true connection. And instead of helping us, it's actually hurting us.

Because, like it or not, real emotions are a *good thing*.

————

The other thing that social media has given us, for better or worse, is a really exceptional outlet for pretending. Which is where catfishing comes into the picture.

Much in the way that it's less stressful to communicate with your mom via email, it's easier to present yourself online as someone more exciting or accomplished. It doesn't take as much effort to exaggerate or lie when you don't have to look someone in the face.

Online, we can pretend that our real lives are glossy and perfect, even—especially—if we are actually unhappy and unsatisfied. Social media is the perfect escape. We can go there every day to pretend for a few minutes—or for countless hours. For some people, the pretending consists simply of acting more popular or active than they really are; for others it's about trying on entire alter egos, and sometimes doing a lot of harm in the process.

I worked on a *Catfish* episode that didn't end up airing that focused on a girl who—for the sake of anonymity—we'll call Monica. In order to boost her self-esteem after a bad relationship ended, Monica began friending beautiful women online in order to steal their online identities—manipulating them into giving her video clips and photos. She'd create convincing new Facebook profiles with that information and use those new fake profiles to befriend yet more women, stealing their photos and identities, and so on.

For years, Monica lived vicariously through these alter egos, whose personae seemed so much more alluring than her own. But it didn't make her any happier. In fact, it made her even more miserable: Not only was she still depressed and lonely, but now she was also disgusted with her own dishonest behavior. She didn't think she was worthy of anyone's friendship.

What struck me when I met her was that her original unhappiness and loneliness could have been resolved long ago had she just put the same energy into improving her life that she had into faking those profiles. She'd wasted not just hours, but years.

When I meet with catfish like Monica on my show, I tell them what most people won't: *Clearly, you want a different version of your life, which is why you created it for yourself on the Internet. So why don't you do it for real?* It's a challenge that applies not only to catfish but also to all of us.

It's easy to say that one of the biggest issues with the Internet is that people can pretend to be someone else. That's a boogeyman everyone can get behind: *Catfish are bad.* But at the core of *that* problem is how we are relating to ourselves in the digital age. The truth is that when you're on social media, you are essentially having a conversation with yourself. We hide, and the result is that we prefer shallow relationships based on 140-character tweets rather than real conversations based on intimacy.

CHAPTER 9

The Myth of the Little White Lie

At this point, you're probably still thinking that the lies catfish tell don't have anything to do with *you*, right?

Wrong.

The truth that no one likes to admit is that we *all* lie online, to varying degrees. Dishonesty in social media is at epidemic levels. Surveys show that 25 percent of all Facebook users admit to lying on their profiles.[6] Teenage girls are even less honest: 70 percent say they lie on Facebook, according to a *Seventeen* magazine survey. And statistics show that up to 80 percent of people who date online are lying about *something* in their profiles—their height, their age, their weight, their favorite band.[7]

There are lots of ways we lie online. The vast majority of these are little white lies, of course—photos that don't quite tell the truth, status updates that pretend at better lives, profiles that exclude unflattering facts, even the perfectly lit high-angle selfie. Social networking almost *encourages* us to fudge things, from the filters we use to make our photos prettier to the way we upgrade our height/weight stats on Match.com or simply exclude certain unfavorable information about our job history on LinkedIn.

But so what? If it's just a little white lie, what's the harm? It's not like you're *catfishing*, right?

Let me stop you right there. Because, as I've learned from making *Catfish*, no one starts catfishing with a big lie. Usually, it's the little white lie that's the gateway drug to the big, bold lie. It's amazing how easily one or two small lies can snowball into something much, much bigger.

I'm not saying that everyone who alters their height and weight on Match.com is going to become a catfish. But it's all part of the online culture of dishonesty in which we're now living, a culture in which the lives that we present to our friends on the Internet are increasingly at odds with the lives that we really lead. And when this dishonesty is at the foundation of our relationships with our friends and our romantic partners, *everyone* suffers.

————

Who do you want to be? If you're anything like me, you are nowhere near your own ideal. Maybe you want to be more successful, or better traveled, or better educated, or plain old ridiculously wealthy. Me? I want to be a leader. I want to be someone people look up to and admire for my accomplishments. I want to feel like I've had a purpose and made a difference in people's lives.

Here's another question: Do you present yourself online as being far closer to those ideals than you are in real life?

We all have ambitions, goals, things about ourselves we want to change and improve. But getting motivated to actually *do* those things is far more difficult. What I see with young people—and I include myself in that group—is a lot of procrastination: a sense of endless time. *I'll get to that someday.* When it comes to things like going to school or really buckling down for some weight loss—the two subjects that the people I encounter on the show lie about the most—a lot of people fail to take that initial step. They may *say* what they want to do, over and over—"I'm going to get my GED and apply to community college. Maybe next year..." "I'm going to start that diet—next week..."—but then they don't do anything about it.

And that's fine. It happens. But what *isn't* fine is posting on your Facebook page that you're already going to school, or that you've already lost the weight. Don't fool yourself: Posting it doesn't make it a reality. Instead, you'll get recognition that you haven't truly earned from your online friends. This is the fantasy projection that I encounter so often with catfish, but it bears repeating for *everyone*. It's the issue at the core of this book. Thanks to social media and our culture of public consumption, the way you are perceived seems so much more important than what you actually are. The Internet lets you get that attention without having to do the hard work.

These kinds of little white lies actually get in the way of achieving what we want. They set up an emotional hurdle that we have to clear. Because due to our fudged digital profiles, we can now receive the same attention that we would get if we'd actually achieved those accomplishments. When we do this, we're getting real attention from real people, so it feels good... temporarily. But eventually that feeling fades and we have no real accomplishment to back it up, so we start to feel crappy again. It's easy to see how this cycle perpetuates itself.

————

Toward the end of season two of *Catfish*, I got to meet Brian, a former marine (episode 208). He'd been introduced to a girl named Jesse online, and they spent three years chatting before planning to meet in person. But on the actual day, he never showed up. It turned out that Brian had PTSD and didn't tell Jesse because he wanted her to believe that he was the happy guy he wanted to be. On the day of their meeting, he'd had a flashback, and had subsequently been arrested for being in possession of a shotgun. And—making matters worse—he was married (though he was separated), another fact that he hadn't wanted to tell Jesse for fear she'd reject him.

Brian wasn't a fake, and he wasn't pretending to be someone radically different from who he really was. His little white lies were lies of omission, wanting to hide the things he was insecure about. But the lies grew in scope the longer he failed to acknowledge them. The outcome of his dishonesty was that once she did get to know him—after they'd finally spent time together—he wasn't who she'd imagined he was. Even though they tried to work it out, their relationship was based on misperceptions, and everything fell apart.

So yes, the lies that we tell online can be obvious—about our appearance or our accomplishments—but often, they are far more subtle. Lies of omission; lies about our emotional state; lies about our vulnerabilities. Lies that are so subtle that we sometimes don't even admit to ourselves that we're lying.

Social media has put an incredible pressure on the Facebook generation. We've made our lives so public to one another, and as a result we feel pressure to live up to a certain ideal version of ourselves. On social media, everyone is happy, and popular, and successful—or, at least, we think we need to look like we are. No matter how well off we are, how thin or pretty, we have our issues and insecurities. But none of that shows up online. We don't like to reveal our weaknesses on social media. We don't want to appear unhappy, or be a drag.

Instead, we all post rose-colored versions of ourselves. We pretend we have more money than we do. We pretend we are popular. We pretend our lives are great. Your status update says *I went to a totally awesome party last night!* It won't mention that you drank too much and puked and humiliated yourself in front of a girl you like. It says *My sorority sisters are the best!* It doesn't say *I feel lonely and don't think they accept me.*

I'm not saying everyone should post about having a bad time. But pretending everything is perfect when it's not doesn't help anyone.

The danger of these kinds of little white lies is that, in projecting the happiness and accomplishments we long for, we're setting impossible standards for ourselves and others to live up to.

———

As I've said, almost none of the catfish that we meet on the show start off by telling big lies. Instead, they start with little lies and escalate from there.

Once you start, it's hard to go back. With every little lie you tell, you dig yourself deeper into the hole.

We can't lie like this without being aware that it's wrong. It breeds self-hatred, since, after all, we *aren't* that ideal self we are presenting online. It's a vicious cycle: The more we go online in order to present ourselves in a certain way, the farther from that reality we'll become. The happier we appear online, the less happy we will be in real life. The more active we are online, the less active we'll be in real life.

CHAPTER 10

Avat-Are You Kidding Me?

How do you set up your online profiles? Maybe you pick a flattering picture of yourself...or a photo of someone else entirely. Maybe you describe yourself...or the person you wish you were. Maybe you tweak your profile with someone specific in mind in order to appeal to them.

Catfish are extreme examples of this—like my own catfish, Angela, who created online personalities that were designed to appeal to my love for bands, ballet, and photography—but we are all guilty of it, to some degree.

Including me. I've done it myself, more times than I can count: picked a photo that hides all my shortcomings or included only part (the most flattering part) of the story of my life. On Facebook, I've been known to look up the profile of someone I've just met to see what they are interested in—books, bands, movies, TV shows—and then, whether I like those things or not, add them to my Facebook page so that when I friend-request that person, they'll see that we have common interests: "Hey, we *both* like *Family Guy*!"

One thing I know for sure: Manipulating your photos and your online profile to "hook" people who wouldn't otherwise be interested in you is not going to improve your life. Sure, you may get a momentary thrill when someone shows an interest in those altered photos. But the truth is, you're setting yourself up for failure.

———

Ashley was an insecure twelve-year-old girl when she met a guy named Mike in a chat room (episode 210). She was really struggling with her weight. As a result, she'd become a kind of recluse, so insecure about her appearance that she wouldn't even allow herself to be photographed at family events. But she did have a Facebook page. And there, she posted photos that she'd run through Photoshop in order to trim herself a little. Nothing dramatic—she didn't pretend that she was radically thinner—but she'd lift her cheekbones, remove her double chin, and post only photos taken at one specific, flattering angle.

But in the meantime, Mike was also overweight, and he was also lying about his appearance. When Ashley asked to see Mike's photos, he sent bogus pictures of some handsome

Abercrombie & Fitch–like model with ridiculous abs. Ashley wasn't stupid. She didn't buy it. But she didn't say anything because she knew her own photos were dishonest, too.

This went on for six years, until we finally met them both. Each of them was terrified to reveal themselves. They never made plans to meet, because they were too embarrassed about their appearances. Instead, they hit a kind of glass ceiling on how close they could get. Luckily Ashley recognized that it was time for some honesty, and she reached out to us. Only when we showed up on their doorsteps did they feel ready to take ownership of their lies.

It didn't go well. They both realized that they'd been dishonest with themselves and each other. And that ended up getting in the way of more than six years of friendship— a beautiful, magical relationship that had been a consistent presence for both of them through some really awful ordeals.

When we left town, it looked like that was going to be the end. Fortunately, though, Ashley and Mike stayed in touch, and their feelings quickly regenerated. Soon, they admitted that they were in love and started moving toward being in a relationship. It was a rare happy ending, but it was also incredibly frustrating: All that time had been wasted. So much *could have been* if those doctored pictures hadn't gotten in the way. (Most devastating of all, Mike ended up dying a few months later, making that wasted time even more tragic.)

Technically, theirs was a catfish story—but it's also not terribly far from what countless other people do every day.

Take a look at the photos on your profile. If you're like me, you often take a picture a half dozen times to make sure you look *exactly* the way you want to before you post it. You add a filter and only post the most flattering photos. It's what everyone does, barring the handful of people who honestly don't care about how they look (they are rare, but they exist, and they tend to be comedians). We believe—and rightfully so—that we'll be judged on how we look. So we do our best to appear put together.

That isn't necessarily a bad thing. But it's something to pay attention to because it's a stepping-stone, a gateway into the realm of Internet identity addiction. Once you start adjusting your photos, what's next? What else don't you like about yourself that you can fix with a few keystrokes?

I hear extreme catfish stories all the time, stories about men and women who told massive lies and duped people for years. But the stories I hear the *most* frequently? They're the everyday minor deceptions, the people who tinker with their pictures. Especially in the world of online dating. I hear these kinds of stories almost every day: "I didn't get catfished, but I'm on PlentyOfFish and every time I go to meet the guy he totally doesn't look like his pictures." Or "It wasn't even him in his photos."

People do this because they know that when you're trying to catch someone's interest online, the most important thing—like it or not—is a picture. After all, if you don't like someone's picture, you're probably not going to click on their profile. People who fudge their photos justify their decision by saying, "It was the only way to get to know the person I was interested in." Maybe they are right. But it doesn't help them in the long term.

As humans, we want to believe that love is blind. That if

someone really loves you, it shouldn't matter what you look like. Looks don't last, and accidents can happen, but love is forever, right? There is no doubt some truth to this, but equally important is the truth that we are beings for whom romantic relationships are based in no small part on physical attraction. It's mammal science. I can't speak for everybody, but in my experience, no matter how much I've wanted to like someone or longed for it to work out, when there's no spark there's just no spark. You can't convince yourself to be attracted to someone.

I've learned this, over and over, from doing *Catfish*: No matter how close two people get online, if one person has lied in their photos, the relationship almost always ends when they meet for the first time. When a catfish is revealed, the hopeful almost never says, "Our relationship isn't about the physical, so your looks don't matter to me." (They also almost never say, "I don't like the way you look"—they're not that cruel.) Instead, they say something about not trusting the other person anymore (which is also true) and then quietly end the relationship.

Ashley and Mike were able to move past their fudged photos, but they were the exception, not the rule, and even then it was a tough hurdle. The truth is that romantic relationships require some physical attraction. Pretending you look different than you really do may help you *meet* someone online, but it won't help you develop a true relationship with them. Because the minute you meet that person in real life (and if you want a real relationship, you *will* have to meet up eventually) they'll know that your photos didn't tell the truth. And that's exactly where things will end: with a lot of wasted time and the potential for a broken heart.

I'M NOT
PERFECT
- BUT -
CONFIDENCE
- IS A -
STATE OF
MIND

(HOLD NEXT TO YOUR FACE + SMILE)

If you tell the truth, you don't have to remember anything.

—Mark Twain

It should go without saying that we should strive to be honest and honorable in everything we do and say, online and off. And it's not like we don't all tell little white lies in real life. (Try this one on and see if it fits: "How do I look today?" "You look *great*!") But online we tend to give ourselves far greater leniency with the truth. We tell ourselves, "I know this isn't true, but what's the difference? It's just my Facebook profile." But Internet life is becoming inextricably linked to (or at the very least, misinterpreted as) real life.

You may think that you bear no resemblance to the catfish on our show, but even the littlest lies can turn around and bite you in the ass. Trust is at the core of everything, so be honest.

Next time you start to fudge your profile data or upload a misleading profile photo, ask yourself: Am I improving my life by doing this? Or am I setting myself up for failure? Instead of hiding who you really are, strive for total honesty, even when it hurts, and use *that* as the launching pad for helping you become the person you want to be.

Only by embracing who you really are can you get the things you really want.

CHAPTER 11

You Are What You Tweet

Rebecca Sedwick was a pretty, normal twelve-year-old girl living in Florida—who just happened to piss off the wrong person. When Rebecca's ex-boyfriend began to date another girl, that girl took offense to Rebecca and began an online smear campaign against her. Soon, up to fifteen kids at Rebecca's school were bullying her, sending her nasty texts and posting taunts on her Facebook page, like "Drink bleach" and "Die."

So she did: In September 2013, she climbed a tower at an abandoned concrete plant and jumped to her death.

A horrible story, and if you read the news with any regularity, you already know that Rebecca was not an anomaly. In the year before her death, at least nine teenagers committed suicide due to cyberbullying. And that's just the tip of the iceberg, the ones who took the fatal step of killing themselves. Untold thousands, maybe even hundreds of thousands, simply live with online cruelty every day.

Bullies are just the obvious and extreme end of a broad spectrum of online unpleasantness. The Internet is jammed with all kinds of haters who think they can do or say anything online without consequences. Consider the trolls, who riddle the landscape of the Internet. Like catfish, they use the anonymity of an online identity, in this case to be mean: They criticize and bully without any accountability, discharging their negativity out into the world. You'll find dozens of trolls in the comments section of every blog, there for no other reason than to piss people off.

Online, we've fostered a culture of negativity where it's considered acceptable (even cool) to say things that are nasty, critical, and downright mean. Almost everyone is guilty of participating in this mentality at some point—whether it's posting a nasty book review on Goodreads, saying something snarky on a friend's Facebook page, or making a catty remark about a stranger's Instagram photo.

It always blows my mind that people follow me on Facebook just to post mean things on my wall—but they do. And this behavior isn't limited to high-profile people like me. Thanks to the Internet, *everyone* encounters haters, no matter who we are or what we do.

Sure, most of the unpleasant things that people say online aren't going to cause someone to kill themselves, but all the negativity still has deep-rooted consequences. It's time to start holding people accountable for their online behavior—and that means starting with ourselves.

Before we go out and start critiquing other people's words and hard work, we need to ask ourselves if we've earned that right by doing anything risky ourselves. Putting yourself out there—being creative—deserves support. It takes a lot of courage. Let's reward *that*, instead of diminishing it.

––––––––

When I was growing up, if you said something mean to someone, you'd either end up in the principal's office or facedown in the dirt, getting your ass kicked. But now kids can be as evil to one another as they want, and then simply turn off the computer and walk away.

> *I think [cell phones] are toxic, especially for kids.... They don't look at people when they talk to them and they don't build empathy. You know, kids are mean, and it's 'cause they're trying it out. They look at a kid and they go, "You're fat," and then they see the kid's face scrunch up and they go, "Oh, that doesn't feel good to make a person do that." But they got to start with doing the mean thing. But when they write "You're fat," then they just go, "Mmm, that was fun, I like that."*
>
> —Louis C.K., comedian, on *Conan*

The Internet is an amazing tool with which we all enjoy the freedom to express ourselves, with almost no legal or social accountability. That's an incredible thing. Most people use this freedom wisely. I am always so excited to hear about people who create amazing online communities in which they connect with people around the world. Many build businesses, raise money for charities, share art and culture...the possibilities are endless. I am inspired daily by the photographs and films posted online by people around the world with messages of positivity and love.

But social media has also given an outlet to millions of kids and adults who were victims of unhappiness, abuse, and bullying themselves, and are now releasing that same aggression on other people.

I've met plenty of bullies over the past few years. And more than one has told me that they believe that they can transfer their negativity. They say things like, "I feel shitty, so someone else should feel shitty, too. That way, I'll have balanced the world and made sure that *everyone* feels shitty."

Awesome logic, right?

Take the case of Mhissy, the first-season catfish I mentioned before. She created a Facebook page for a fake guy in order to mess with the head of Jasmine, a girl she once had a relationship with and who she felt had betrayed her. Mhissy seemed like a pretty unpleasant person, but when we dug down, we discovered her logic. She was hurting, she felt like she had no control over her life and the way she'd been treated, and so she thought to herself, "Jasmine hurt me. I want to hurt her back. That way I can make sure that she feels the same way I feel."

Hers was a one-to-one direct relationship, but a lot of people who go online to vent their frustration spread their negativity anywhere they can. For example: "My dad fucked me up, so I want to fuck someone else up; it doesn't matter who it is." It's a kind of pass-the-buck mentality—the inverse of paying it forward.

In our worst moments, we're all capable of this kind of thinking. If we're not careful, we can seed nastiness and hate everywhere we go. When we go online, it's just so incredibly easy to use social media as an outlet for all of our frustrations, to give in to our most unpleasant impulses without any consequence. The challenge we all face is learning how to spin our negativity into something more worthwhile. (More—much more—on that in a few chapters.)

We have all been haters at one point or another. No matter how nice of a person you are, odds are you've given in to a bad mood at some point and impulsively posted something unkind, written something anonymously, or gotten involved in an online flame war.

Look, we all do it. But I think we should try to be more careful.

Everything you say online you are saying to *someone*. That post didn't write itself; a robot didn't take that photo. There's a person behind every single image and word on the Internet, a person who took the time to create and share their feelings and ideas. So even though, in an instant, with zero accountability, you can make a negative comment—don't. Even a remark that feels insignificant to you *is* significant to that real person. A person like you. Just because you don't have to look them in the eyes doesn't mean it doesn't hurt.

I've come up with a few simple, commonsense guidelines for online accountability. If everyone tried to live by the following rules, the Internet would be a much nicer—and more productive—place.

- Remember that you're talking to real people. Don't say it online if you wouldn't say it to someone's face.
- Find a constructive way to express yourself rather than defaulting to a snarky shorthand. Say what you really mean, but say it nicely. Craft a thoughtful opinion.
- Before you hit "post" on anything, read your post out loud. Think about how you'd feel if someone said the same thing to you.
- Don't post anonymously as a way to vent. It's cowardly.
- Don't pick a fight just for the sake of entertainment.

RESOURCES

Sometimes, no matter how positive you try to be, the hate that you encounter online is just too much to shoulder on your own. Bullied teens like Rebecca Sedwick need serious emotional support, and I'm aware that in these cases, telling someone to try to spin their experience into something positive isn't going to cut it.

Fortunately, there are support groups out there that exist specifically to help kids who are bullied. Sites like www.endcyberbullying.org offer online counseling, and the National Suicide Prevention Lifeline has a great website and a hotline that's available 24/7.

And for those on the other side of that equation—the bullies—there's a great organization called Leave Out Violence (LOVE) that is focusing on helping teens channel their anger into more productive outlets. So you're pissed off? Don't join a gang or bully someone online. LOVE teaches teens to express their emotions through photojournalism, poetry, creative writing, and more.

CHAPTER 12

Less Is More (Except When It Comes to Chest Hair)

So, you've got an online crush. She likes you. You like her. You've chatted. You've texted. You've tweeted. You've "liked" every photo she's ever posted on her Instagram. It's *tru luv 4evr*. Now what?

It's time to take a picture of your junk, right?

Wrong.

At some point in the past few years, courtship took a left turn. Everyone from politicians (I'm looking at you, former congressman Anthony Weiner) to athletes (go ahead, Google "Olympic pole vaulter") to tabloid celebrities (Kanye, Blake Lively, Kesha; the list goes on and on)—not to mention teenagers everywhere—decided that the best way to show someone that you like them is to take a naked selfie. A hand-bra shot, sent via text message or Snapchat, became the modern equivalent of going to first base. Dick shots? More popular than love letters.

There are a lot of good arguments against sexting and naked selfies—the demise of romance and intrigue is a good place to start—but the number one reason that you shouldn't send them? You never know where they'll end up.

Consider what happened to four teenage girls in Etiwanda, California. All four of them had sent naked photos to their boyfriends; those boyfriends then passed them on to their friends. One of those friends posted the pictures online and bragged about it on Twitter. Pretty soon the naked photos were a trending Twitter topic. Those "private" shots the girls had sent to the guys they'd liked? Not just their entire high school, but the *whole Internet* was looking at them.[8]

Every day, it seems like there's a story about someone whose revealing selfies and sexts went viral—whether it's the Miss Teen USA who was blackmailed by a guy who hacked her social media accounts and stole naked photos of her[9] or the fourteen-year-old who got charged with child pornography after sending a naked photo of his ex-girlfriend to everyone he knew.[10]

The lesson here: No matter how private you may believe that picture is, you never know where it will end up. You may *think* you're in a relationship with someone you love and trust, but things go wrong. People lose their minds. It happens all the time. Seriously, I've seen some people go cray cray for real. And then they have pictures of you. It's just a mouse click to revenge porn sites, where scorned lovers go to post the naked selfies that their exes gave them.

Think it'll never happen to you? Think again. Remember those naked photos that I sent of myself to my online "girl-friend" Megan? Well, I would soon learn that someone else entirely had them, someone whom I didn't exactly want to have them. I feel a twinge of mortification every time I think about that. To this day, I worry that somehow those photos will turn up somewhere embarrassing and very public.

According to a study by McAfee, 13 percent of all adults have had their personal content leaked on the Internet without their permission. The same study showed that 10 percent

(There was another photo without the deer head.)

of all exes threaten to publish their former lovers' naked photos online, and a majority of those go through with it.[11]

It can get even worse, believe it or not. A growing number of teenagers are ending up as victims of "sextortion." Here's how it works: A girl meets a "cute guy" online (actually, a child predator) who offers to send her a naked photo in exchange for one back. As soon as he gets her picture, he blackmails her. She needs to keep sending him sexy pictures—or even perform live sex acts over a webcam—or he'll send her pictures to everyone she knows. Her school, her parents, her boss. So she keeps doing it.

It's horrifying, and growing in scope every year.

If there's one rule of social media to always remember, it's this: Everything that you post, text, and tweet can be used against you in the future. On the Internet, there is no real privacy. Before you do *anything* online—sexting, compromising selfies, photos, and comments of all kinds—remember that it's going to live there forever, for potentially anyone to see. Your friends. Your teachers. Your boss. Your future friends, teachers, and bosses. Total strangers. *Your mom.*

———

Sexy pictures are the most obvious no-no, but those aren't the only kind of shortsighted photos posted on social media. It blows my mind how often I see Instagram photos of people getting drunk, doing drugs, and smoking weed, including high-profile celebrities like Rihanna and Justin Bieber. People think they're untouchable online, but they aren't—just ask the fraternity in Florida that got itself suspended for hawking drugs on its Facebook page,[12] or the Milwaukee teen who was arrested after police saw an online video of him getting high,[13] or the young mom who was charged with a misdemeanor after posting a "joke" photo of her baby holding a bong.[14]

Even things that seem innocuous can come back to haunt you. Consider the woman who got fired from her job after making some critical comments about her boss on her Facebook page;[15] or the high school teacher who was fired after the school board came across her Facebook vacation photos, featuring a trip to the Guinness Brewery.[16]

Instead of being your own personal, private playground, your social media pages are actually a vast, permanent resource for any authority figure that wants information about you. And these days, *everyone* does. If you are applying for a job, trust me: Those employers will Google the hell out of you before they hire you. Do you think they'll want to hire someone whose Facebook page is full of stories about their love of Adderall and Goldschläger, or their disgust for their current place of employment?

When you apply for college, the first thing admissions officers now do is plug your name into Facebook. What happens when they come across a gallery of red-cup party pics of you—even if it's on your friend's page? If they have to choose between you and thirty thousand other applicants, they'll choose the applicant who *wasn't* getting wasted in their photos. Every time.

And think about your health insurance. Sure, you may not be worrying about this yet, but at some point, you will. Those companies don't have to rely on your own self-reported health questionnaire anymore, not when your Instagram feed is a better measure of how you're really living your life. It's not out of the realm of plausibility that they would jack up the price of insurance for someone whose photographs show him smoking cigarettes, drinking heavily, and eating junk food.

"But Nev," you say, "I have great privacy settings! No one but my friends can see my photos on Facebook." Great—but friendships and relationships fall apart, and when people get angry or jealous, ugly things happen. Digital information is incredibly easy to copy and disseminate. Incriminating photos of all kinds are a very popular revenge currency.

Even if your friends *are* one hundred percent permanently

trustworthy, accounts still get hacked. Phones get lost and stolen every day. You don't want some fourteen-year-old computer nerd getting into a cab and finding your boyfriend's phone loaded with naked photos of your hoo-ha.

"Okay, fine, Nev," you say. "I'll just use Snapchat." But there is no guarantee that that picture really has been erased forever. The person who got your selfie or the snapshot of you doing drugs can always screen-grab your photo, for starters. Plus, you just sent an image millions of miles through space, bouncing across hard drives and servers. Trust me: It still exists. It's been saved *somewhere*.

Once you publish something on the Internet, you lose ownership. The information you share over your free phone apps isn't private. Those app companies *own* it. They have access to it. Your posts on social media websites? Some of these sites have privacy policies that allow them to use those posts however they want—including using your face or words to endorse something.

Heck, even the government can watch you, if it chooses to. The NSA tracks everyone's emails, texts, and social media. Get noticed for the wrong reasons, and they'll start digging up that digital file with your name on it and every beer bong photo you've ever taken. Think that sounds paranoid? Maybe. But the government has already admitted that they do it.[17]

Did you know that lawmakers can subpoena your social media account? One suspect in a murder case was found guilty in part because he'd described himself on his Myspace page as an "outlaw" and a "criminal."[18] And Facebook status updates and comments are increasingly being used as evidence of cheating in divorce proceedings.[19]

Sure, these are pretty extreme examples that probably

won't ever be relevant to you, my law-abiding friend. Still, no matter how strong you keep your privacy controls, if you ever wind up in the public eye—not just because you did something wrong, but because you become famous or even decide to run for public office (you never know!)—you can bet that someone's going to go digging. The last thing you want the whole world to see is the first thing that will be used against you.

———————

Fame has really changed my approach to social media. It's why I practice consideration and awareness of everything I post before I post it. It's why I'm more respectful of other people's privacy. Because everything I say online now is potentially material that anybody could use. An offhand tweet might seem insignificant to a couple hundred friends, but in my case, it's hundreds of thousands. My tweets get picked and published in newspapers. The news media uses my tweets as a source. When I put something online, I'm essentially publishing it, signing my name to it, and making a statement.

As a result, I'm very sensitive about what I say online. I want everything that I say and post, every link that I share, to be something I can really stand behind. I never want to post anything that will be offensive, or hurtful, or shameful, or embarrassing.

In my case, because I'm a public figure, my posts can have a tremendous effect on my career and reputation. But even if you're not a public figure, you have to consider the moments when you *will* be worried about your career and reputation. Because those moments *will* happen, whether you anticipate them or not, even if it's just the manager of the local 7-Eleven Googling you before they hire you.

We live in a time when we feel compelled to document

everything we do—good and bad—without stopping to think about the ramifications. We mindlessly post photos and comments all day long, every day. We are so concerned about constantly updating our feeds—making sure we always look popular, busy, and fun—that we don't think about the consequences of the particular photograph we've just uploaded.

The outcome? Our lives, good and bad, are out there for everyone to examine, exploit, and criticize.

So what should *you* do about it?

First, realize that your online identity is very much part of your real-life identity. It's not *"just my Facebook page, where I get to be silly and funny and free with my friends."* Nope. Not anymore. That social media persona is the *first* thing that any stranger is going to encounter when they look you up online.

In other words, it's time to start being mindful of your image on the Internet. Before you post a photo, take thirty seconds to think about it. Ask yourself: What would my parents think if they saw this picture? What would my school think? My boss? Could this affect me in the future? How does this reflect on my personality? Could this hurt my reputation? Could it be considered offensive by someone?

If it could be construed as having a negative reflection on you—don't post it.

Look, I don't want you to entirely avoid expressing yourself; I'm not saying that you need to be squeaky clean and opinion free. I just want to make sure that you can justify everything you post and that you are willing to stand behind your words and images. That you consciously control your online image, rather than letting it control you.

The same goes for photos that your friends post. It's nearly impossible to prevent yourself from ending up in other people's photos these days; I'm not suggesting that you avoid all camera phones, because if you did, you'd never leave your house. But if a photo of you drinking, smoking, or partying— doing *anything* compromising—turns up on someone else's Facebook page, *untag yourself.* And, more important, pick up the phone and have a conversation with that friend and maybe ask them to take it down. It may not even be a picture; it might just be an inappropriate message. If someone makes an unflattering comment on your Facebook page, reach out to them and ask them not to do it anymore.

Yeah, I know. No fun. But they'll understand. We need to start a global conversation about the importance of privacy, and the best person to start it is you.

(Of course, it goes without saying—don't post compromising pictures of other people on your Facebook page without asking them, either. Yes, I know that you're going to tag your friends in your photos—without that habit, social media would come to a screeching halt—but be considerate and respectful.)

A second maxim to live by? The more you value your privacy, the more people will value you. Set your privacy controls on all your social media accounts at the maximum security levels. You should be sharing your photos *only* with people you really know. (And by that I mean people you have met in person and have a real-world relationship with.) Hold people to a high standard and make sure they have earned your trust and deserve to see inside your life. Remember that you don't have to whore yourself out to be popular on the Internet, especially not at the risk of humiliation.

As I've come to realize, privacy is more valuable than you think. Remember what Andy Warhol said? *Everyone wants their fifteen minutes of fame*. Well, that may have been true for the past few decades, but the world is changing fast. We are becoming such a public society that I think in the future, everyone will want their fifteen minutes of anonymity. The more wealthy and successful we are, the less accessible we'll be. That's how status will be determined.

Already, the people *I* pay most attention to online are the ones who are the most mysterious. We all know there is nothing more frustrating and exciting than seeing a cute guy or girl "like" one of your photos on Instagram, but when you go to check out their profile: Alas! It's private. It makes me want to know more. It means that woman values her privacy; she doesn't let just anybody into her life. Her exclusivity is a self-respect that makes me respect her more.

Everyone wants to be part of the club that's exclusive. So make your life exclusive. And invite only people who are worthy.

———

Okay, one final note. Ladies: Keep your tops on. That hand-bra shot is not gonna make him like you any more than he already does. Guys: No more dick pics. There's nothing romantic about a photo of your junk.

Seriously, you're not doing yourself any favors by sending pictures of yourself naked. Sure, it's easy to do. But in romance, less is more. Subtlety is *powerful*. When it comes to love, people are interested in what they can't see. When you reveal yourself in full in a photo, there's no more mystery. You've showed your cards. Shot your wad. (Figuratively *and* literally.)

A better way to be sexy and flirtatious is to be coy, to reveal only a little bit at a time. A sexy picture of your eyes is more

Dear _____ ,

You are one of the most _____ people

in my _____ .

Every time I see you, I think to myself

_____ , that _____ is
WOW / OMG / DAMN / UGH [CHOOSE ONE]

_____ .
OUT OF THIS WORLD / SO SEXY / INSPIRING / KINDA WEIRD [CHOOSE ONE]

You always make me _____ when
LAUGH / SMILE / RELAX / FART [CHOOSE ONE]

I am _____ .
UPSET / ANNOYED / HUNGRY / GASSY [CHOOSE ONE]

The best part of knowing you is that I always have a

_____to go on _____
CRAZY / STUPID / SILLY / SPONTANEOUS [CHOOSE ONE]

adventures with.

Looking forward to the next time you _____ me.

Let's get together soon for a _____ .
COFFEE / DATE / SNUGGLE / RUN [CHOOSE ONE]

_____ ,
BEST / ;) / XOXO / LOVE [CHOOSE ONE]

_____

FOLD HERE

A SPECIAL NOTE FOR YOU

AND HERE

intimate and exciting than a blurry photo of you standing naked in front of a bedroom mirror.

Guys, if you really want to impress a girl and tell her that you like her, here are a few things that are far superior to that junk shot you were considering:

- Give her an actual handwritten love note.
- Buy or hand-pick flowers and leave them on her doorstep.
- Buy her an iTunes movie rental and invite her to watch it with you.
- Make her a personalized Spotify radio station.
- Send a cool picture you took of something *besides* yourself.
- Show up outside her dorm with a boom box on your shoulders.

Better yet, rather than sending her a text message, call her on the phone. Listen to her voice. I know—crazy, right? But more can be accomplished in a ten-second phone conversation than in hours of texting.

And your best option of all? Go out. On a date. A *real* date. It seems insane that I should have to tell people to meet each other in person, but judging by what I've seen over the past few years, I do. Social media has become a fallback for all human interactions—including sexual ones—but face-to-face communication is always the superior choice. I'll never forget the feeling of sitting at a movie with a girl and building up the courage to reach over and hold her hand for the first time. The exhilaration of having her turn to me and smile might just be one of the best feelings in the world.

CHAPTER 13

Love at First Skype; Or, Nev's Rules for Online Dating

If you're alive, single, and under the age of, oh, say, seventy-five, odds are good that you've looked for love online. Forty percent of all single people are using online dating services these days.[20] A full *third* of all married couples now meet online.[21] According to one MTV study,[22] traffic to the top ten online dating sites has actually tripled in the past few years. And that's just dating sites; even people who aren't using those sites are meeting and dating online—often through Facebook or other online communities.

Online dating may take all kinds of forms now—from people who hunt for mates on JDate, to people who fall in love while blasting aliens together in *Halo*, to people who spend their days flirting with strangers on Facebook—but the one common factor is how much time and energy it can consume. Online flirtation can suck up huge swaths of the day. Relationships that would have ended quickly if the people involved actually *met* in person get drawn out for weeks or months or years instead.

Clearly, the game has changed. And we still don't know the rules.

If you'll indulge me, I'd like to propose some.

NEV'S RULES FOR
ONLINE DATING

Putting Up a Dating Profile

Congratulations. You've decided to take control of your love life; you're going to set up a profile on Match / OkCupid / eHarmony / FarmersOnly / PlentyOfFish / whatever launched this month. Here are a few things to keep in mind.

1. Do not lie in your profile. Period. Don't lie about your height, your weight, your job, your car, your college, or the name of your pet iguana. You're just setting up yourself—and the person you meet—for disappointment.
2. Use pictures that look like what you *actually* look like. Provide a full body shot, not just the most flattering angle shot. Choose a few good snaps rather than uploading a whole photo album: It's about quality, not quantity.
3. Don't use your name—especially your full name—in your profile username. Don't provide an address or phone number, either. Duh.
4. If you like something obscure—a quirky band, an interesting book, a sport, or a hobby—list it in your profile. Don't be embarrassed. You never know who else might be totally into naked tennis, too. It might even be the thing that brings you together.
5. Conversely, don't pretend you like things that you don't actually like. It will make for an awkward conversation when your date brings it up. *So, you're into football too, huh? What did you think of the second-round NFL draft picks?* Uh…

6. When you read other people's profiles, be open-minded to their interests. Don't discount them because of something they enjoy. Sure, maybe you don't like dubstep music now, but you might someday.

7. Be honest, but don't give away too much. If you are overly revealing on your dating profile (or your Facebook page, for that matter), it's easy for someone to study you and prepare a perfectly crafted strategy to appeal to you. This might seem great at first, but if that's not really who they are—especially if they're just doing it to get you into bed—you're facing a lot of heartbreak down the road. You don't want a stranger to play on your weaknesses. (We've all seen *There's Something About Mary*, right?)

8. Expect the best but prepare for the worst. That's an old adage that holds particularly true in this situation. There are a lot of weird people out there. If you date online, you *will* meet some of them. But you might also meet the man or woman of your dreams...And who knows? Your soul mate may even end up *being* one of those weirdos.

When You Meet Someone Interesting

Okay, your profile is up on a dating website. You've been pinged by a cute guy or girl. They have sent you a few flirty messages; you've flirted back. Mutual interest is clear. Now what?

1. Do your research. Hit up Google, Facebook, Twitter. See what their public profile is. Make sure they aren't a

felon or married. But also don't take an offhand Reddit post from five years ago too seriously. In other words, get an overall vibe on that person, but don't sweat the tiny details.

2. Trust, but verify. Don't be afraid to do your background research on this person, and double-check what they've told you. (Refer to chapter 5, "How to Identify a Catfish.") Keep in mind, though, that there's a difference between a background check for safety and stalking someone: Get enough information to verify this person's identity, but don't try to learn *everything* about them before you meet them. Leave some room to get to know them organically.

3. Do not Facebook friend them. Instead, wait until *after* you've met them to make sure they are deserving of your "friend"-ship. You don't want a total stranger to have access to your photos and private profile.

4. Skype before meeting. Save everyone some time and make sure the person is who they say they are. This is a good chance too to make sure there's some physical attraction. There is more to attraction, after all, than looks—there's the sound of a person's voice, the way they carry themselves, body language, and so on. (On a related note: Make sure your Skype name isn't your full name.)

5. And last but definitely not least: Don't just online date, *offline* date. Meet the person as soon as possible. Remember, the Internet is the means of *finding* the person, not dating them. Give every relationship a deadline to actually meet in person. Don't be afraid to give the other person an ultimatum.

VIRTUAL CONTRACEPTION

→ You should do a certain amount of research — at least 10 minutes or so is enough ┆ on any person you're getting involved with ONLINE, to protect yourself.

MAX IS THE GREYTIST

The First Time You Meet

Congratulations! This guy seems to be who he says he is. He's asked you out. You've made a plan to meet. *Now* things get interesting.

1. Meet in a public place, tell people you are going to be there, and keep your phone on. Have a friend do a check-in halfway through the date.
2. Don't discount someone just because you don't feel an immediate connection when you meet them. It might be the beginning of a friendship. Or they might introduce you to someone else.
3. Remember to remain casual. Yes, you've Googled this person. You've seen their social media pages. You know a lot about them. But don't let that affect your first date. It doesn't mean you are already intimate or that you're signing up for a long-term commitment the first time you meet in person. Let a first date be a first date.
4. Give yourself an out. Tell your date that you're meeting a friend later or that you have an appointment; if you are enjoying yourself, you can always blow the "appointment" off.

5. Don't overdo it. Just like your online identity can sometimes be hard to live up to, the way you present yourself
   on that first date can be tough to maintain if you go overboard. Look your best, of course, but look like *you*.

Forging Ahead

So, you actually like this guy. There's a physical attraction. He
seems like he's into you, too. Your phone is on fire with text
messages from him. Now what?

1. Take it slow. *Take it slow. Take it slow.* I can't repeat it
   enough. Go out again. And again. Get to know each
   other. Don't decide someone is your soul mate after one
   date. Don't change your relationship status. Don't send
   a naked selfie before you've gotten engaged. (Matter of
   fact, don't send one at all. Ever.)
2. You've gone on three dates and you're still feeling it?
   Great; now it's time to become Facebook friends, follow each other's Twitter feeds, and start "liking" each
   other's Instagram photos.
3. But don't let an online relationship turn into a full-time job.
   Flirting on Facebook with a guy you are dating—or even just
   like—should not take up more than ten minutes a day.
4. Don't obsess over the small things, like Instagram "likes"
   and Facebook comments. Yes, it's fun to exchange
   "likes," but they are not important in the long run. Texts,
   "likes," and comments are the easiest, lowest form of attention; they're what people do while they're doing something else (even sitting on the toilet). They don't really
   matter. So don't worry about how much attention you're
   getting from the tip of their finger (unless you're naked

together, but that's a different story). The *real* gestures are what show you they care: A phone call. Inviting you out on a date. Introducing you to their friends. Sending you a present. Leaving you a note. *This* is the stuff worth obsessing over, not messages on your Facebook wall.

I can't reiterate it enough: Online dating is just a conduit to offline dating. Even if you can't meet in person—say, you live in different cities—bring the relationship into the real world as soon as you can. Skype. Send each other letters. Talk to their friends on the phone. Send each other mixtapes.

Perhaps most importantly, don't assume that just because a new relationship isn't working out exactly as you'd hoped that you should give up. Don't assume that Mr. Perfect is out there online somewhere waiting for you. Real love is a product of trust. Trust takes work. Relationships require commitment, compromise, and consideration. Just because we now have access to millions of people around the world doesn't mean that when we find a special person it will immediately be "happily ever after."

Look, I'm not a love expert. I'm just trying to share what I've learned. And although I can make a list of rules for you, I know that there are no hard and fast rules for love. No two relationships are the same: Sometimes you have to go with your gut, feel things through, and take risks. But take the right risks.

PART THREE

How to Live and Love Offline, Too

You know me from my TV show. Maybe you've seen the documentary, too. But the version you know of me is, in many ways, the exact opposite of the person I used to be.

I don't have all the answers to life. I'm not a psychologist. Just like you, I constantly struggle with fear, insecurity, and questions about how to make my relationships work.

But one thing I do know is that I spent many years of my life heading in a direction that I didn't want, and I was finally able—with a tremendous amount of work and struggle—to take control of the big wheel of my ship, stop the negative momentum, and turn my life around. My world may not be perfect now—no one's is—but it's a vast improvement on what it was. What I did that's fairly unique was simply spend a lot of time thinking and talking about myself, both in therapy and with my friends and family.

So while I can't tell you exactly what to do with your life, I know what *I* did, and I can share what I learned along the way.

And, thanks to my work on *Catfish*, I've also listened to a lot of other young people talk about their feelings and thoughts and ideas. While other people go to med school or law school, I've been doing my fieldwork in friend school. I've spent years exploring how the Internet has become a crucial part of the fabric of friendships, relationships, and communication. I've witnessed firsthand how it can be both wonderful and terrible at once.

Yes, I know I've talked a lot about the negative aspects of social media so far in this book, but I do believe that it can be terrific. For creative people, it offers an unbelievable platform that otherwise doesn't exist, a place to share your talent and passion and to connect with people and potentially even be discovered. One of my favorite places online is Vine, a totally unbiased democratic platform where you can achieve status by earning it through your work. Some of my closest friends now are people I've met on Vine—filmmakers and musicians and comedians like Nicholas Megalis and Jerome Jarre (who now works on *The Ellen DeGeneres Show* because of Vine).

Social media is also an incredible resource for communities, as we saw during the Arab Spring in the Middle East. It gives a voice to people who are otherwise voiceless. It allows people to fight oppression and garner support for events that will alter the course of history. In the United States, it's a serious outlet for otherwise marginalized points of view, allowing people to easily share and shed light on issues of great importance without the construct and filter of mainstream media.

And while I still love the charm and satisfaction of a physical photograph, there's no question that social media has made sharing photos and experiences with your friends and family infinitely easier and more immediate.

That said, I'm trying to start an honest discussion about how social media is affecting our lives.

I don't want to scream at everyone to "get off the Internet." But that's what the TV show *Catfish* is ultimately about—encouraging people to stop looking for excitement and love on the Internet, and to instead turn off their computers and look around them. It doesn't matter whether you live on the East Coast or West Coast; a small town or a big city; in Paris, Texas, or Paris, France—everywhere that we have access to social media, people are just not spending enough time in real life anymore.

What I've learned over the past few years is that all people are looking for a deeper connection. We're looking for happiness, success, self-acceptance, and love, but despite all the time we're spending on social media, we're not finding those things there.

This section is about where you *will* find them.

CHAPTER 14

My Catfish Story, Part Three

By the time Rel, Henry, and I arrived in the Upper Peninsula of Michigan, just a short drive out from Ishpeming, we were exhausted. We'd already stopped by Megan's horse farm only to discover that it was vacant. We'd found my postcards in the mailbox, marked *Return to sender.*

In the middle of the night, we finally collapsed at a weird little motel near Gladstone, right on some lake. By this point, I knew that Megan was lying to me about more than just her music. I wasn't sure how to feel anymore. In the days since I'd accused her of sending me those fake songs, our relationship had been strained. And yet, I *still* wasn't anticipating anything really bad when I met her. I *still* thought my mutual attraction with Megan would provide for an interesting encounter. I thought the whole family would be surprised and excited to meet me. After all, they'd talked for eight months about how they thought I was the greatest, how much they wanted to meet me, how much they wanted me to meet Abby.

If this goes well, I thought, *I could end up spending time here. Or being in a relationship with her and bringing her home.* I was still optimistic, despite everything that had happened the previous week.

But a nagging voice in the back of my mind kept saying, *If she's lying about the music and the horse farm...who's to say she's not lying about being the girl in the pictures?* I did my best to push this thought out of my mind.

Rel, Henry, and I stayed up late that night, talking through the possibilities of what might happen the next day. I revealed my last and most embarrassing card—I read out loud my sext message history with Megan. I knew the texts were silly and cheesy. I even felt a little guilty about them, because she was nineteen and a virgin. It was the last thing I wanted to share with my brother. But there was no turning back; tomorrow was going to be a defining moment, no matter what happened. I figured I might as well put all my cards on the table. Within hours, this intimate correspondence would either be a mortifying moment in my past or a part of a burgeoning future.

The following morning, we got up early to make the final drive to Ishpeming. Before we showed up on Angela and Abby's doorstep, we made a few final—and illuminating—stops in town. We wanted to have as much information as possible before meeting the family so we could determine whether what they were saying to us was true.

First, we stopped at the UPS store from which Abby's paintings had been shipped, where the nice woman who worked there told us that sure, she knew Angela—*She's always shipping her paintings to New York City. I even bought a few from her myself.* Huh?

Then we hit up the town art gallery, the store where Abby's paintings were represented by the dealer and family friend Tim Hobbins. No one knew who he was; no one had ever heard of Abby.

We drove by the old JCPenney store that Abby and her family were supposedly renovating as her personal art gallery; it was empty, with a FOR SALE sign in the window.

More and more pieces of the story were starting to fall apart. It was beginning to seem like *Angela* was the family artist, not Abby. And yet, although it was crazy that Angela had been lying to me about this, that part of the story really wasn't so important to me anymore. I was there for Megan.

Still, by the time we arrived at Angela's house—a pretty two-story wood-sided Victorian with a garden full of flowers—I had suspended any expectations about my relationship with Megan. I felt like I'd pressed a mute button on my feelings. Instead, I'd taken off my lover hat and put on my detective hat. I was on alert: I was looking for the truth, hoping to be as objective and unbiased as I could be without upsetting or hurting anybody.

After we parked across the street from Angela's house, Rel and Henry put a mic on me and hid it underneath my shirt. As I walked up to Angela's front door, carrying a bouquet of wildflowers, followed by Rel with a camera, I felt a certain heart-pounding thrill that can only be achieved by going out on the edge and being a little daring.

The woman who opened the door was Angela, but not the Angela I knew. Instead of the angular, exotic-looking sylph I'd seen in the photos and paintings, the Angela I faced now was plain, a bit frumpy, and bespectacled, although friendly looking. Whereas "my" Angela looked way younger than forty, this Angela looked older. The only point of resemblance was the incredibly long hair dangling down her back.

"Megan's not here," this strange Angela blurted almost immediately. "Abby's not here." But she hugged us, introduced us to her husband, Vince—who also bore no resemblance to the youthful, hunky Vince we'd met online—and continued: "Nice to see you. But you guys shouldn't have come."

It was immediately clear that nothing was as we'd been led to believe. Abby, Alex, Ryan, and Megan weren't at the house, although two severely disabled twin boys were—Ronald and Anthony, the latter clearly not the Anthony I'd met on Facebook. Angela was obviously their caretaker, and she was gentle and kind with them, despite their need for constant attention. The house was full of paintings, although it wasn't clear who had painted them. Oh, and by the way—Angela had ovarian cancer. She was starting chemotherapy that week, she told us.

For the better part of that day, Angela did her best to convince us that the absent Megan was simply in Gladstone (at the house we already knew was for sale) along with her brothers. Both she and I called Megan's cell phone over and over, leaving urgent messages, but none were returned.

Abby was easier to locate. Angela drove us out to the lake, where Abby and a friend were staying at a beach house. Abby was the only person we'd met who actually matched the photos we'd seen of her—but she seemed to have no clue what we were talking about when we asked her about her painting. Instead, she seemed like a normal eight-year-old girl, giggly and awkward and primarily interested in goofing around with her friend.

Finally, I asked Abby how often she saw her older sister, Megan. "I never get to talk to her or anything and I don't know what she looks like anymore," she said.

At that moment, it finally dawned on me that Megan, as I knew her, didn't exist. That in fact, Angela *was* Megan. In fact, Angela was everyone. She was Abby; she was Alex; she was Ryan, Tim Hobbins, Noelle. She was every single one of the fourteen Ishpeming friends and family members I had communicated with over the past eight months. She'd written every single one of the 1,500 emails that I'd received. This entire world that I'd been so deeply embroiled in? My online love affair? It existed only in this lonely woman's head.

I didn't confront Angela with the truth. I needed to digest it first. Instead, we spent a bucolic afternoon on the beach with the kids, making small talk and avoiding the hard truth that all of us knew would eventually need to be acknowledged. We finished the day with a promise to come by again.

Back at the hotel, Rel, Henry, and I tried to parse the facts in order to nail down the truth. Meanwhile, my phone was finally lighting up with text messages from Megan: *Are you seriously at my mom's? Stay there. I'm coming home!*

The next morning, one last text message arrived, supposedly from an inpatient rehab facility called Dawn Farms:

I can't come home, Nev. I came here with Alex to get help. I have a drinking problem and it's serious. By now you know my mom is very ill. I can't continue to do this and neither can Alex. I have my farm up for sale. Sorry I've disappointed you. Peace, Meg.

I wanted to believe it. But by this point, I couldn't.

Later that morning, we met Angela and Abby at a stable where Abby took horse riding lessons. As Abby rode in circles around the paddock, I confronted Angela. "I'd like to meet the real Angela," I said gently, as Angela began to cry. "There's nothing to be upset about. You have a great imagination. It's pretty remarkable."

She confessed to everything. Yes, there was a Megan, she told me: her nineteen-year-old daughter, who was in fact in rehab at Dawn Farms. "Megan's" life was based on her daughter's life, Angela told me, although the real Megan hadn't ever communicated with me and didn't know that I existed. The girl in the photographs was a family friend, she said. Later, I'd discover that the photos were actually of a Vancouver, Washington–based model and photographer named Aimee Gonzales, who had never met Angela; the rest of the people in the pictures whom I'd "met" on Facebook were actually Aimee's husband and friends. Angela had downloaded Aimee's entire photo gallery off Myspace and ModelMayhem.com, relabeled the photos, and repurposed them in order to fashion an alternate universe for herself.

The paintings? They were Angela's, not Abby's. My correspondences with Abby about art technique? That was Angela, too. I'd never actually emailed with Abby, although the one (very) brief phone conversation I'd had with her had been legitimate. Alex, Ryan, Tim, Noelle, and the rest simply didn't exist in any form. And Vince knew nothing about his wife's Facebook activities—he'd been told that I was just Angela's art patron, her best customer, which, being incredibly supportive of Angela's painting, Vince simply took at face value.

That night, after Angela's confession, Henry, Rel, and I sat in our hotel room and discussed what we wanted to ask Angela when we could have a quiet moment with her. We went over the previous eight months and put together a list of questions. For Rel and Henry, the question was, *How had she done it?* For me, it was, *Why had she done it?*

Why? Well, it wasn't so hard to figure out. In Angela's day-to-day life, she was a struggling homemaker dealing with the all-consuming challenges of disabled children and regretting the life decisions that had left her artistic ambitions behind—but on Facebook, she was able to live out those dreams and be the person she'd always wanted to be.

"I guess I knew in the back of my mind that this would happen," she told me on our last day there. "I thought, 'I don't want to lose this friendship, no matter what. But if I'm lying, is that really a friendship anyway?' So it got harder. And I really thought you'd just end up hating me."

But I didn't hate her. Instead, I ended up spending four days with Angela and her family, four surprisingly enjoyable days. Her family dynamic was amazing: Vince was passionate about Angela's artwork, Abby was adorable, and Angela's commitment to her kids was admirable. Angela pleasantly agreed to be in Rel and Henry's documentary. We left hopeful that we would stay in touch and be friendly.

During those four days, I was able to roll my shock and disappointment and disbelief about the loss of Megan under the table. There were moments when it would hit me that I'd actually been having an online romance with Angela, but I managed to disconnect myself emotionally. I was wearing a lot of hats simultaneously: I was an impassive documentarian working on getting this amazing material on film; a baffled lover who had just had the rug pulled out from under him; an empathetic friend trying to fully understand the woman whom I'd been so close to without knowing her at all.

It wasn't until I got back to New York City that the sadness hit me. Suddenly, I was terribly lonely. The steady stream of emails and text messages and funny posts and Gchats that had filled my days were gone. It was very quickly apparent just how much time and energy I'd been investing in Megan and her family. I had all this free time I didn't know what to do with. In the center of my life, there was a void.

I *missed* Megan.

Which maybe explains why I was so quick to pin my hopes on an alternate Megan, the "real" Megan at Dawn Farms whom Angela had told me about. When we left Michigan, Angela had promised to put us in touch with her real daughter; sure enough, within the week I'd received an email from a girl named Megan telling me how sorry she was that her mom had done what she had. She was available to give me any answers I might be looking for. Her pictures, though bearing no resemblance to the provocative Megan I'd fallen for, depicted an appealingly cute, tomboyish equestrienne.

I felt like I knew her—even though I didn't. Somewhere, in the back of my head, I began to conflate *this* Megan with the Megan I'd believed in, a faint hope that compelled me to start emailing with this new girl on a near-daily basis. She told me stories about her troubled mother, Angela, and gave me some insights into her family's tumultuous life. I wondered—if the whole character I'd fallen in love with was based on *this* Megan's reality, then maybe *she* was the dynamic, active, sexy girl I'd fallen for, and maybe now that I'd actually found her, my correspondence with her could turn into something more. As crazy as that sounds. I was reaching for something to hang on to. I was feeling lost and sad.

Unfortunately, despite the steady stream of chats and emails, it was proving hard to get Megan on the phone, thanks to Dawn Farms' restrictions on phone use. For two weeks we made aborted efforts to speak in person before it finally dawned on me that this relationship with New Megan was starting to feel suspiciously like my former relationship with Old Megan. At that point, I called Dawn Farms directly and discovered that, although they wouldn't confirm the names of their patients, one thing they *could* confirm was that their patients had no Internet access. None at all. In other words, there was no way I could have been communicating with a Megan at Dawn Farms.

Angela had lied again. And she'd also lied about the cancer, as I found out after I called to confront her. She was emotional and apologetic, explaining that there really *was* a Megan who was her daughter, but Angela hadn't spoken to her in years; that the real Megan was the result of a bad high school relationship; that Angela had been a stripper with a drug problem when she was young; and that Megan had been raised entirely by her father.

"My grasp on sanity is a thin thread these days," Angela wrote me.

At that point I started to really feel used. I could no longer justify why I was still talking to this person. I'd made every effort to be as accepting and generous as possible, and yet she chose dishonesty again and again. No one had ever lied to me like that before; I felt betrayed and disenfranchised. The low feeling turned into anger, fury that Angela had abused my trust and wasted my time. Perhaps this was a much-needed dose of my own medicine. To finally know the confusion and disappointment of being lied to and hurt; of trusting somebody only to have them deceive you again.

For too long, I'd been living my life with one foot out the door, too heavily involved in an alternate—and, as I now knew, totally imaginary—reality in Michigan. It was time to start focusing on my life in New York again.

So I reached out and got back together with Katie. I threw myself into helping Rel and Henry finish the documentary by providing every email I'd ever exchanged with Angela,

recalling stories, and facilitating interviews with all the people in my life who had been affected by our relationship. I
told the story of Angela over and over, at dinner parties and
gatherings with friends. I relived the experience on a daily
basis, hearing about it, thinking about it, and reflecting on it.

Every day I felt like I had more insight into what had happened to me. And yet I still felt lost and confused, unclear as
to what I should be doing with my life. It wasn't until the documentary was complete that I began to see a bigger picture,
and the positive outcome of my catfish experience grew clear.

———

It took over a year for Rel and Henry to get a finished version
of the documentary *Catfish* together, but once they did, the
feedback was immediate. They partnered with two amazing
producers, Andrew Jarecki and Marc Smerling, and took it to
Sundance, where it sold almost immediately. I was surprised
to realize that with the success of the movie came a small
amount of celebrity for me. Because I was the guy in the film,
I was suddenly interesting and desirable. It felt like a lucky
break.

And yet I was still at sea; especially because Katie and I
had broken up after Sundance yet again, this time for good.
(It was my call this time, and for a pretty shortsighted reason: I was excited by the prospect of being the star of a movie
and wanted to be single so that I could fully absorb the attention I was getting.) But as feedback on the documentary
started to come in, I was surprised by how people responded
specifically to my behavior in the film. Viewers would tell
me that I'd shown real compassion for Angela; they were
impressed by my empathy. It was strange to have my choices

Left to right: Marc Smerling, me, Ariel (Rel) Schulman, Zac Stuart-Pontier, Henry Joost, Andrew Jarecki and experiences analyzed and reviewed—and given *positive* reviews—especially at a time when I wasn't feeling particularly present in my own life.

The emails started to trickle in after Sundance, and then, after the film was released in movie theaters, the trickle turned into a flood. The sheer volume of stories similar to my own stunned me. People were looking to me for answers, hoping I could help them understand what had happened to them. They saw me as a beacon, shining through a murky fog of confusion and dishonesty.

Throughout my life I'd always felt that I would eventually find *something*—or perhaps that *something* would find me—and everything would suddenly *click*. I would know in that moment that *this* was what I'd been waiting for, working toward.

Well, I was finally at that moment.

It dawned on me that my calling—my niche, my purpose—was to serve as some sort of mediator. I could be a leader of the vital conversation about how life and relationships are changing now that we spend so much time online. My experience with Angela—and, more importantly, the process of incessantly discussing and dissecting that experience—had led me toward some deeper understanding of myself and my choices, but also of the choices we are all making in the social media age.

I found that what I could bring to this discussion—what I had brought to Angela—was empathy. *I'd been there.* I'd been on Facebook since it launched, yet even as I grew more and more "connected" with the world online, I'd still been searching for and struggling with purpose, identity, sexuality, self-esteem, and happiness. I may never have catfished anyone, but I also knew that I wasn't always honest online. I knew firsthand how hard it was to evolve as a human being—to be present, positive, accomplished, and engaged; to be kind and generous—while spending so much time on the Internet.

I still struggle with these things. I'm still figuring life out; still learning what it all means; and even now, sorting out my feelings about the whole Angela experience. Like everybody else, I'm hurting and confused. Even though I now have a life that a lot of people would dream of having, that doesn't change how I feel inside. I'm constantly trying to move toward being the person I really want to be.

But what I learned—through my own experiences and through the stories that I've heard during the past few years of *Catfish: The TV Show*—is that we all need to take a minute to really think about the choices we are making. And not just about the choices we make on the Internet. The specific challenges of living and loving in the age of social media aren't just about the things we're doing online—they are, even more critically, about the things we're doing *offline*.

Before we can live happier, healthier lives in the digital realm, we need to take a look at the bigger picture of our lives. Only once we step away from the Internet and start living in real life will we be able to find what we really want: love, connection, and self-fulfillment.

CHAPTER 15

Repeat After Me...

Repeat after me: *I am awesome.* And you are. You have the potential to do great things. No matter who you are, what you look like, your background or your sexual preference or the balance of your bank account: The only person holding you back is *you.* I want you to feel great. I know you can.

The first step toward that greatness is being happy with yourself, and to get there you must be honest with yourself and others about who you are.

Consider Heather, who we met on the last episode of our second season (episode 215). She was an insecure girl, struggling with her weight, who had gone on PlentyOfFish and—with a friend—created a fake profile of a beautiful woman named Claire in order to test her friend's husband's fidelity. As Claire, Heather was messaged by a guy named Mike. They chatted and seemed to have a real connection, and within a week Heather had confessed who she really was. But when Mike saw Heather's real photos, he blew her off. Not only was he upset about her lie, he simply wasn't attracted to her.

Wounded, Heather created a second fake profile—using pictures of another girl—and pursued Mike again. As Caroline, she had an online relationship with Mike for almost a year and a half. She pretended to have cancer in order to avoid meeting him, even though she lived just a few miles away. Her obsession with him was so complete that she would drive by his house and tell him about it later, even leave notes on his car.

Heather felt that she had been unfairly judged: Mike had liked her before he saw her picture. Why should it matter what she looked like? But the consequence was that she ended up wasting eighteen months of her life pursuing a guy who had already made it clear he wasn't interested in her. And in the meantime, she missed out on pursuing guys who *could* have been interested in her.

Heather's big issue with herself was the way she looked. She dealt with that by pretending to look like someone else. But if she'd used that time and energy trying to get in shape, she could have found happiness inside herself. She could have set a goal to achieve the fitness level she wanted, rather than hatching a plot to hook a guy who simply wasn't attracted to her.

(To Heather's credit, after she was exposed, she decided to change her eating habits, go to a therapist, and start a video blog as a form of self-expression. Those are exactly the right steps to take—it's just too bad that she had to mess with Mike's head for a year and a half before taking them.)

The most powerful thing you can do is learn to love yourself, to embrace and accept who you really are.

You don't have to be thin and rich and stunningly beautiful to be happy with yourself, either. We've all met those people who aren't conventionally attractive, or who carry an extra ten or fifty or even a hundred pounds on their frame, or who are dead broke and wearing shabby clothes—and yet who walk into a room and *own* it. It's because they are happy with themselves, and they exude confidence. They don't believe that their "shortcomings" are shortcomings at all; they know that they've got something special going on. People are drawn to that like moths to a flame.

We all have weaknesses—aspects of ourselves that we believe are hard to love. They can be physical or emotional. Some of these are even things that we will never be able to change—physical disabilities, family background, and so forth. Hating yourself because of these things is a waste of time. If, instead, you can accept and embrace those weaknesses, you might even be able to put them to work for you.

Take me, for example. I was diagnosed with ADHD when I was very young. It was a big problem for me in school—my hyperactivity got me in all kinds of trouble. I was terrible at doing homework. I was kicked out of three different schools. I was constantly seeking attention, trying to be the class clown. I wasn't particularly easygoing or pleasant to be around. It kept a lot of people away.

I'm also a tiny bit OCD (obsessive-compulsive), with very high attention to detail. I don't have compulsions or weird superstitions, but I am hyperaware and sensitive to my surroundings, and I want my things to be organized and clean at all times. (You could eat off the floor of my house. I'm not kidding.) I know how I want things to be and have a hard time trusting people to live up to my standards.

For a long time, I took Adderall to cope with these issues. I went to therapy (lots and lots and lots of therapy). But at a certain point, I decided to stop. I was finally functioning well in my day-to-day life. And rather than trying to change what was at the core of who I was, I decided to make those "flaws" work for me. I embraced that I was sort of OCD, kind of hyperactive, and had a problem with paying attention, and I created a lifestyle for myself that made use of those things.

Sure, I was constantly distracted. But I was also really good at multitasking and focusing on tiny details. When it came to choosing friends and work colleagues, I knew what I was good at—practical matters, day-to-day chores, tasks—so I put my personality to use and teamed up with people who were much more patient and big-picture than me. My chosen partners, like Rel and Henry, were creative and needed someone like me to help them manage the smaller stuff so they could focus on the overarching issues. The things I couldn't do, I delegated.

I'm not going to pretend that I'm thrilled about having ADHD and OCD, but I am very comfortable with them now. I know how to make them work for me instead of against me. I know how to see my flaws as advantages, to see how they set me apart from other people and appreciate that.

———

Of course you can be confident and happy with exactly who you are, flaws and all. You *should* be. But *finding* that confidence can take work, real work. Confidence comes from within. Some people have it naturally, but a lot of people don't.

Maybe you're reading this right now and thinking that I'm just spoon-feeding you that sound bite we've all heard a million times before: *"You're special just the way you are!"* I'm not. The self-loathing you live with every day isn't going to suddenly go away, no matter how many times someone tells you to love yourself the way you are. Nothing you hate about yourself is going to magically fix itself.

So what if you can't accept and embrace yourself the way you are? The answer is simple: Change yourself to be the person you want to be.

Almost everyone has something about themselves that they don't like, something they'd like to change. Want to hear another one of mine? I have hyperhidrosis, which is a fancy way of saying I get really sweaty. I'm terribly self-conscious about it. I worry about how I smell, and I hate ruining my shirts. Especially on TV, it looks awful. So guess what? I started getting Botox. In my armpits. It stops the sweating entirely. (Yeah, call me vain, but let me tell you, wet armpits are gross.)

So ask yourself: What's preventing you from being happy with yourself? What's that issue that's getting in the way of your life? Identify what your issue or vulnerability is. And then, if you can't embrace it, attack it! Challenge it! No matter what you do, face it head on. *Face your fears.*

It's going to take real action. If you don't have the confidence to love yourself exactly the way you are, flaws and all, you can't just *will* that confidence into existence. You can't *think* your way to being happy. You have to *pursue* that confidence, taking the steps to turn yourself into the person you most want to be. Whether it means going to therapy, or doing community service, or joining AA, or getting a makeover, or signing up for boot camp, or taking further education classes, confidence comes from knowing that you're constantly improving yourself.

It can take a lot of work. You have to invest energy every day toward your goal, whether it's maintaining a physical appearance, a lifestyle, or a psychological presence that you feel good about. That requires things like exercise, diet, cultural exposure and conversation, and informing yourself so that you can be actively involved with the world around you. It means working hard, having a good job, earning money, getting an education. Put in the effort, though, and you'll feel a hell of a lot better than you did when you were just sitting in your room, hating yourself and feeling terrible.

Self-acceptance is a challenge. But as my girlfriend, Shanee, wisely puts it, "*Life* is a challenge. We are born into this thing to be tested, and you can't avoid the obstacles that you'll come across. You need to overcome them. You need to put in the work every day. That's the way you grow as a human being."

The best way to find love is not to pretend that you look or live like someone else; it's to make yourself into the person you want to be. When you're comfortable with yourself, people *will* like you. What Heather learned, through the eighteen months of her relationship with Mike, is that you can't change other people. You can only change yourself.

————

Metaphor time, people.

For more than five years, I walked around in pain. I'm talking about physical pain—my back and neck were really stiff and uncomfortable, all the time. I went to physical therapy, but they couldn't fix it, so I figured it was muscle tension related to stress. Frankly, I was afraid the doctors were going to tell me something terrible—that I had a chronic ailment or something that required surgery—and I didn't want to hear it. So instead of dealing with it, I decided to ignore it. For years.

Then last year, I pulled a muscle in my back, and it hurt so badly that I ended up having to get an MRI. After the doctors examined the results, they informed me that I had arthritic discs in my back. It's a common problem, easy to fix with exercise and stretching.

So now I know what I need to do to fix it. That doesn't

mean I'm gonna do my stretches every day. (I often don't, to my own detriment.) But at least I know that there's a solution, and I can pursue it.

A lot of people walk around in a general malaise. We put off seeking the proper help or admitting the real problem because we don't want to deal with the potential diagnosis. We need to understand what is making us unhappy, but we are afraid of hearing the truth.

Instead, we ignore our unhappiness, distract ourselves, or manifest our issues in ways that aren't productive—whether by wasting time on social media, catfishing, binge eating, or drowning ourselves in drugs and alcohol. But, as they say in AA, the first step toward recovery is admitting that you have a problem. It's all about accepting your issues, embracing them, and facing the truth: *I am unhappy because of X.*

Unfortunately, there is no MRI for the heart. No X-ray for sadness. It's not always simple to locate the source of your dissatisfaction. But there are lots of other ways to diagnose your unhappiness, and it all starts with finding outside help.

I'm serious here—*get outside help.*

Maybe you've heard this before, but here's another metaphor: Think of yourself as a car. You need gas, fuel, and oil. When things are broken, you need to get them fixed, but you can't always fix those things yourself. You aren't a mechanic; nor should you be. Like a broken-down car, you can't simply *will* yourself to be repaired: You need proper professional attention, or you won't drive.

When you are unhappy with something about yourself, and you can't find the solution on your own, seek out the proper mechanic, whether it's in books, from professionals, or from friends. Prescription drugs. Exercise. A therapist. A life counselor. A wardrobe stylist. Whatever it is that's bothering you about yourself, there's someone who can help you resolve it. Find someone to talk to—express that sadness. Don't just internalize it. People around you might have dealt with similar problems in their own lives and might have insights or advice to offer.

And here's the best thing you can do: Use your feelings to create something. Take that energy and *do stuff* with it. Make art. Write. You need to engage with your sadness. Go ahead and express it, whether in a journal or on a blog or through photography or paintings. It will make you feel better. Instead of numbing your pain with drugs, alcohol, social media, and other distractions, convert it: Transform it into something of substance.

There's a John Lennon quote I love: "Life is what happens to you while you're busy making other plans." If you're constantly distracting yourself rather than putting in the real work needed to accomplish something, you're never going to be satisfied. Just ask any catfish who has ever been on my show. No number of "likes" or "friends" is ever going to fill you with the sense of self and confidence you're seeking.

Instead, look at yourself in the mirror and commit to bringing about the change you need.

THE TRUTH IS

I ~FEEL~

_____

(PLEASE FILL IN THE BLANK)

CHAPTER 16

Friends versus "Friends"

Here's a surprising fact: I am not on Facebook. Yeah, I know. Hard to believe.

I *do* still have a fan page there, but I turned my personal Facebook page off in 2012. After years of spending hours on Facebook every day—a lot of them digitally pursuing girls—I decided that I was done wasting so much time. Yeah, sure, I had thousands of "friends" on Facebook—but were they *really* friends? Were they worth all the hours I was spending keeping up with them?

Nope.

I'd been an average Facebook user for years—which means I'd been spending far too much time on the site. Still, until the movie *Catfish* came out, I'd mostly been using it to keep in touch with my real-life friends. But after the film was released, I started getting a ton of friend requests from strangers. At first, I loved it. *This is great!* I thought. *So many people like me!* And in fact, many of the messages I received did end up leading to the TV show, as people used Facebook to share their catfishing stories with me.

But as my Facebook friend list began to grow and fill with people I didn't know in real life, I realized I wasn't using Facebook to communicate with my true friends anymore. I was using it to chat with "friends" I'd never met and to pursue the cute girls who were friending and messaging me. Some days,

I spent hours on Facebook, chatting with girls, looking up strangers' pages, commenting on the photos of people who lived across the country. Ultimately I got to the point where I had *too* many friends—I'd hit Facebook's limit, and no one could friend me anymore.

By November of 2012, I was simply tired of the distraction of Facebook. I just didn't have the time anymore—I was too busy actually *doing* something for the first time in years. I was producing a TV show! I had a new career! And I realized I didn't want the temptation of being distracted by strangers anymore. I wanted to put all my attention into my actual real-world relationships. Instead of wasting hours every day messaging girls I'd never met (and probably never would), I wanted to spend time with the people who mattered in my day-to-day life. The people I really loved.

In the age of social media, we've come to believe that it's a good thing to have hundreds—even thousands—of online friends. We've redefined the term *friend* to mean anyone who has ever clicked a button to acknowledge our existence. But the truth is that friendship—real friendship—is hard work. And avoiding that hard work by nurturing online friendships instead isn't going to make us happy in the long run.

———

If you're young and involved in social media, you probably already know how much of a time-suck online "friend"-ship can be these days. But if you aren't, here's a quick primer on how online relationships work.

First, someone you don't know starts following you on Twitter, or Instagram, or Facebook. They respond to something that you've tweeted, or they tag you in a post. To let them know that you saw what they did and that you appreciate their attention, you go to *their* Instagram or Twitter or Facebook feed and "favorite" or "like" one of their photos or tweets or status updates. This lets them know that you've checked them out, too. The farther back you look in their feed, the more interest you express in them.

Now multiply that times dozens—even hundreds—of people.

If you're under the age of twenty-five, this is quite likely what you are doing *all day long.* (Yes, *you*, I'm looking at you. I'm looking at *you*, and *you*, and *me*, and *them*, and all of us— we're all complicit.) Every spare moment you aren't absolutely required to apply your full attention to something else, there you are on Instagram and Twitter and Facebook and a dozen other social media sites, posting and "liking" and retweeting. You do it in class. You do it driving. You do it on the toilet. It's an all-consuming, reciprocal game: If someone does it to you, you're expected to do it back, and then they are expected to do it back again. And so on. Until you're spending all day long "liking" and tagging and "poking" and commenting and retweeting, trying to keep up with the countless people who are "liking" and tagging and "poking" and commenting and retweeting *you*.

And you don't even know most of these people!

I'd love to blame social media tools for the shallow connections and massive waste of time plaguing modern life, but the truth is that we as a society are responsible for the mire we find ourselves in. We've taken the tools that companies like Facebook and Twitter gave us and completely lost self-control. As a result, social media is kind of like quicksand: The more we thrash around, the deeper we sink, until we get pulled all the way under and we drown. I know because I was starting to drown, too, until I made a conscious choice to change the way I was spending my time and energy.

These days we have a heightened sense of how connected we are. After all, we can measure exactly how popular we are from minute to minute, quantified by the number of "friends" we have. I see people judging their worth by the number of likes they get on photos, declaring it a good day if something they posted garnered more than fifty likes. Or if a tweet got twenty retweets. We are measuring our value entirely on the attention we get on social media. Instead of thinking about our real lives and what we may or may not be accomplishing there, we worry about whether we have more Facebook friends than everyone else in our class.

For centuries, popularity was a nebulous thing, hard to quantify, hard to achieve. It's actually quite difficult to be popular in real life. Just ask anyone who's survived high school. But online you can be wildly popular very easily. There's an exact metric with which to judge it. And if your real self isn't popular with a lot of people, well, you can pretend to be someone you're not—you can curate out the bad and highlight the good. It's easy to have a gazillion friends! So much easier than real life!

But what this does is isolate us and keep us from having real connections. We can see that every day when we look around us—people sitting at restaurants, looking down at their phones instead of the person across the table; friends who are together and yet not together because both of them are too busy tweeting to talk. We are spending more time milking our online popularity than interacting with the people who actually know us.

Take a wild guess which one matters more, in the long term.

———

I'd like to pause right here for a mild attack on Facebook Inc. for hijacking the word *friend*.

It used to mean something if someone was your friend. You didn't get friend requests. Someone didn't *ask* to be your friend. They just *became* your friend because you spent time with them and showed them that you cared. They were your friend because they were present in your life, active in your happiness, and supportive of your ambitions. They were accountable to you.

But then Facebook came along and decided that all that's required of someone to be your friend is a mere click of a mouse. Instead of having shared life experiences with you as part of a balanced exchange of give and take, now your "friends" simply consume your photos and status updates. They are witnesses to your life, not participants in it. Your life online is just another content stream that distracts and entertains the people you are "friends" with, and your identity is like another channel for people to flip through, admire, or judge.

How is that in any way a friendship?

Let's just admit it: Being a "friend" with someone on social media means nothing unless you actually know that person, and know them well. Maybe social media was initially conceived as a tremendous way to share photos and stay in touch with the people you know and love. Certainly some people still use it like that. And that's great! That's what it should be used for! But something vital shifted when sites like Facebook and Twitter crossed the line into *suggesting* friends for you, people you "may know" simply because you and they share a friend. Suddenly, these sites and apps were cross-pollinating groups of friends to get you even more invested in the tools they provide. (From their business perspective, when you have more content to consume and browse through, you spend more time on that app/website and they can sell more advertising.)

Don't get me wrong: It's not bad to be connected to other people. But the way we are communicating is unbelievably shallow—it's become quantity over quality. You can be "liked" by thousands online and yet have very few friends in real life. I see it all the time. It's an escape from reality, a means by which people who are unhappy are able to justify the time they spend isolating themselves. They can claim that they are online "making friends"—but these people are not their friends. They don't know anything real about them.

> *Have you ever had that moment when you're updating your status and you realize that every status update is just a variation on a single request: "Would someone please acknowledge me?"*
> —Marc Maron, comedian, in his book
> *Attempting Normal*

So why are real-life friendships important, anyway? Why can't you replace a few real-life friends with a thousand online ones?

Let's try something right now. Go and post on your Facebook page that you're sick and could really use some soup.

Then see how many people call you on the way to your house with a hot bowl of chicken noodle soup.

I am willing to bet that you won't get many responses, and if you do, they will be people posting "Feel better" or a sad face. If someone does show up at your door with soup, it's probably someone who is already a close friend in the real world. Your mom, your best friend, your neighbor. Am I right?

That's real friendship. Isn't that one person who shows up with soup far more valuable than the hundreds of other people you spend your days dithering around with online? Stop wasting your time with those "friends"—and spend more time working on your relationship with the person who is going to show up at your door.

Here's how friendship works: There's a finite amount of connection that any one person can have with the world around them. You get to choose how to distribute that time and energy. It's like your bank account of friendship. If you have a girlfriend or boyfriend, you'll give a certain value of time and energy there. And then you have your family and your best friends, who take up more value. At that point, your account is pretty depleted. So if you want to make more friends, you'll have to take value away somewhere else. You can't spread the same amount of time and energy across an infinite number of friendships.

But the Internet tells us that we *can* be friends with *lots* of people, because each friendship requires an incredibly low level of investment. If you spend six hours a day online, you can say you are "friends" with thousands of people. That's a sexy, alluring concept for many of us—who doesn't want to be able to say that they have lots of friends? But in real life that's impossible. There's just not enough in your friendship bank account.

In other words, maintaining a friendship with someone on Facebook requires almost zero effort. In real life, the moment you stop actively working on someone's friendship, that connection begins to weaken. No wonder so many people are trying to take the easy way out.

A *real* friend is someone you can count on day or night—to help carry a couch down five flights of stairs or pick you up on the road when your car breaks down. You only need two or three of them. (Unless none of them have a car, in which case you need a fourth.) I can count my true friends on one hand.

When I think about what real friendship is, I think about the time my brother, Rel, was driving up to Boston. Halfway up I-95, he pulled over at a Mobil/McDonald's rest stop and parked in a yellow no-parking zone, over a gutter, so he could dash in and pee. As he was getting out of the car, he accidentally dropped the car keys in the gutter. No key = stuck in the middle of nowhere.

Luckily, Rel had a spare key in his apartment. He called me and asked me to drive into New York City from Westchester County (where I lived) and retrieve it. So I did—I drove into the city, got the key, drove another hour and a half up I-95 in order to deliver it, and then turned around and drove right back home again. Did I mention that it was ten thirty at night when he called?

But of course I was going to do it. It was for *Rel*—my brother and best friend. There was only one person in the world who was going to help him like that: me. Anyone else would have said, "It's too late; can you wait until the morning?" or "Get a tow," or they would have looked at the clock and rolled their eyes and simply not answered the phone.

I know that Rel would have done the same thing for me, if

I were in his shoes. And I also know that there are only a few people in existence whom I could count on that way. I cherish every one of them. And trust me when I say that *none* of them are "friends" that I met on Facebook.

YOU DON'T NEED A CERTAIN NUMBER OF FRIENDS, JUST A NUMBER OF FRIENDS YOU CAN BE CERTAIN OF

I've had a lot of low periods in my life (see: getting kicked out of pretty much every school I ever attended), but there's no question in my mind that the rock bottom—the absolute nadir—was the time I broke my best friend's face.

Mark had been my best friend since kindergarten. When I was kicked out of grammar school for clogging the toilets with toilet paper? He was kicked out with me. In junior high, we briefly lost touch when we went to different schools, but we reconnected in high school and grew even tighter.

When I was at Sarah Lawrence, he was a short drive away at a different university, studying film. Soon, we'd formed a little film collective together with our brothers and were making short experimental films. By the end of my sophomore year, in 2004, we had been invited to be the crew for a film that the Neistat brothers, documentary filmmakers we'd met through mutual friends, were filming in Connecticut—a documentary about their ninety-three-year-old tap-dancing grandmother.[23] We jumped at the opportunity.

After a week on location, with the four of us crashing in one tiny hotel room and working around the clock, we were all exhausted and testy. But that's still no excuse for what happened on the next day of the shoot. We were at a Radio Shack when Mark picked up a megaphone and accidentally blasted it right in my face. Annoyed, I smacked him upside the head with an open palm and stormed out of the store. In retaliation, he followed me and smacked *me* upside the head from behind.

I was caught off guard, my ears ringing. I turned and looked at him. I remember thinking, "Just walk away. Cool down." But I didn't. Instead, I slugged him with all my might, right in the face.

There was blood everywhere. I knew immediately that I'd fucked up terribly, and I tried to help him, but it was too late. The damage was done. I'd broken his nose and fractured his skull. He was rushed off to the hospital.

After we got back from Connecticut, Rel sat me down. "I'm always going to be your brother. I'll always be there for you, and I'll always love you," he said. "But I do not *like* you right now. I don't want to be friends with you in your current state." He went on to explain that I was a bully, always aggressive in my interactions with other people—not so much physically, as I was with Mark, but also with my humor and my sexuality. My jokes were usually put-downs. When I hit on women, I didn't know when to stop. And he didn't want to be around that anymore.

Ever since I was a kid, Rel had been the most important person in my life: not just my brother, but my most important friend. I'd always looked up to him and often felt inferior to him. Aside from Mark, Rel's friends had been my only real friends when I was a kid. So when he rejected me, I was shaken to my core. *Oh God, I've lost my brother*, I thought. *Even he can't pretend to like me anymore.*

It was the worst moment of my life. But when I look back at it now, I can see that it was also the most important. It shook me up. Thanks to this moment of truth from Rel, I began the long and difficult process of redefining who I was and what friendship really meant to me. I realized that because of my behavior, I'd lost the two friends who meant the most to me—Mark and Rel. It was my own fault. And if I wanted to earn their friendship again—if I wanted to learn how to be a *good* friend—I needed to do some serious rethinking.

In retrospect, I'm so happy that I had someone who was willing to be honest with me, even if it meant hurting me deeply. His lecture was the spark I needed to really start doing the hard work of becoming the better person that I am today.

It didn't happen overnight, not by any means. I may have recognized that I no longer wanted to be the jester character who makes jokes at everyone else's expense, but it took me years to make that epiphany a reality. For a long time, I just licked my wounds and sulked. But ultimately I began to formulate a plan. Thanks to Rel, I started to understand both how to be a friend and what I should be looking for in a friend. And I learned the hard way that the best way for me to grow was to surround myself with people who inspired and challenged me, and who taught me things I didn't already know.

So I decided that if I could earn the trust and affection of creative, talented, meaningful people again—people like Rel and Mark—then I would have become a decent and meaningful person myself. My goal was to be the person whom the people I admired most would *want* to be friends with.

———

My transformation started like this:

My dad was a ballet groupie. Not long after I went off to college, he got involved in a summer ballet workshop called the Morris Center Project, led by Benjamin Millepied (the talented dancer who choreographed *Black Swan*, now married to Natalie Portman), that brought dancers and choreographers together for three weeks of creative exploration on Long Island. My dad hosted three dancers at his house; he invited me to come and observe them as they rehearsed. It was fun and inspiring. It reminded me of my childhood love of dance, a passion that I'd forgotten about over the years.

Soon, I was a total ballet groupie as well. My dad and I would go to the ballet as often as we could, serving as a de facto cheering section for our favorite dancers. We'd deliver flowers to the girls' dressing rooms, make NY City Ballet T-shirts, and host annual open-invitation Christmas parties for the ballet companies. We were the Ballet Boys.

After I broke Mark's face and Rel subsequently broke up with me, my awesome dad had a moment of intuition that I needed a little focus. He got me a job working on that summer's choreography workshop as a documentary filmmaker. For three weeks, I was a part of something exciting, and I even had a film at the end to prove what I'd done. I worked hard to be a positive, useful guy, and as a result, I ended up earning my place in a very small and cool group of ballet friends. For the first time, I was included because I'd proven myself worthy.

It was a turning point: I had the epiphany that I wanted to be a part of something. I'd found an art and lifestyle that I was passionate about; a group of people that I really admired and that I wanted to admire me. They inspired me to better myself—and that's the most important quality in a friend. Even if I was still feeling insecure and confused after the fall-out of my friendships with Mark and Rel, I understood that by associating myself with people who were doing good things, I too could be involved with something great.

So I started showing up at ballet events, offering my services as a photographer and videographer. I crashed NY City Ballet galas, took pictures, and posted them on my nightlife website, TheContactSheet.com. I talked my way into any rehearsal space or ballet institution having a performance and offered my filmmaking services at no cost. I'd show up and say, "I don't see anyone making a film of your rehearsals; mind if I shoot a piece?"

I wanted to be *the* New York City dance photojournalist. And soon, I was. Not long after the fight with Mark, I got kicked out of Sarah Lawrence (like I said, my epiphany took time to set in and affect my actions), and within a few years, I was right at the heart of the ballet community, capturing it. I was the guy with the camera. Just being around these talented dancers whom I respected and admired—observing their hard work and commitment to their art—made me feel better about myself. I challenged myself to be more productive, committed, and creative. I believed that my pictures would someday be important because the artists I was photographing were going to be important.

When you find something you are passionate about, *commit to it*. Make it your whole life. Take risks. Put yourself in front of the people who are already successful at that thing. That's what I did, and it paid off. My friendship with the New York City Ballet dancers ultimately led to a creative collaboration called *Opus Jazz*, a film we shot with those dancers in the summer of 2007. That led to a job with the Morphoses dance company, which led to a project I did with Juilliard. In turn, that led to real, inspiring friendships. It led to romantic relationships with talented ballet dancers. And it led to one of my dance photographs being published in the *New York Sun*, a photo that ultimately resulted in my relationship with Angela.

———

I'd found a great new community of friends in the ballet world. And yet, the most important person to me—the person whose respect I valued above all others'—was still Rel.

By my early twenties, I had turned my life into a full-time quest to be the kind of person Rel would want to be friends with again. My first epiphany, courtesy of my new ballet community? I understood that choosing where I wanted to physically locate myself and trying to be in service to the people whom I admired could play a big part in achieving my goals. So I set a goal: to get Rel and his cool new business partner, Henry, to move into a shared office space with me. I figured that would be a first step toward being closer to them. And if they were spending time with me, I could better show them the positive parts of my personality, traits and qualities that I'd been working on. I wanted to be useful to them.

So I rented an office space I couldn't at all afford on a cool New York street that was crawling with interesting creative people (including the Neistat brothers, Lena Dunham, and Red Bucket Films, to name a few), and I asked them to move in. It was a huge risk—way beyond my budget, and if they'd said no, I would have been screwed. Fortunately, they agreed.

And then I went to work making myself indispensable to them. I bought ink for our printer, did tech support, cleaned up after parties—anything I could to give them more time and space for their creative filmmaking. I volunteered to assist on their projects. I humbled myself. I paid my dues, and it worked. Within a year or two, I'd earned my way into their inner circle. (It's a funny thing: When you start taking actions consistent with who you want to be, one day you realize you've become that person.) We began working on projects together, even hanging out after work. We were, once again, real *friends*.

A successful friend once gave me a piece of advice that really stuck with me. "Don't set a budget for yourself that reflects your means," he said. "Instead, set a budget for the means by which you'd like to live. And then find a way to make it happen." In other words, start to live the life that you *want* to live and *then* figure out a way to make it work. Push yourself. Rather than renting the apartment that sucks, rent the apartment that costs a little bit more and force yourself to hustle to pay for it. Maybe you'll look for a better-paying job or take a few extra risks that will help expand your life. His point was that you have to challenge yourself, otherwise you'll never grow.

I'm not saying that you should go rack up a whole bunch of credit card debt. Bad idea. You shouldn't take these words as carte blanche to go out and buy that Lamborghini you covet. But stretching, in the right context, is a good thing. Just make sure that you follow through, work hard, and are fully aware of the reality of what you're taking on.

This advice certainly worked for me. I rented that office that I couldn't afford, because I knew that I wanted Rel and Henry nearby. I created an opportunity by taking a reasonable risk, and as a result shared an office with people who would become my very good friends and—ultimately—end up making a documentary about my burgeoning online relationship with a family in Ishpeming, Michigan. If I had been sitting at any other desk, without Rel and Henry behind me, that strange experience may simply have gone undocumented and may have just been dinner conversation instead of the defining moment of my life and career.

But the most important lesson that I took away from my breakup and makeup with Rel was about humility. You need to acknowledge that there are people who are more talented than you, more sophisticated, more mature. You need to challenge yourself to meet them at their level. You don't have to like all the same things, share the same opinions, or be in the same sorority or fraternity—after all, the best friendships are a give-and-take. But sometimes the best way to make someone a friend is to recognize when they need something that you can provide. So there's a cool person you admire? Aspire to be their friend. Find a way to involve yourself in their life. Be at their service. Figure out what they need and how you can help them.

And often, simply by having access to them, you'll build a friendship that will force you to grow into a better person.

––––––––

If I were to pick one quality that is absolutely the most important one to have in a friend, hands down I'd pick honesty. That's the final lesson I learned from Rel's tough love. We all need to surround ourselves with good people who not only inspire us, but also will tell us the truth, no matter what.

I was incredibly lucky to have family and friends who were willing to tell me the difficult things I needed to hear in order to grow into a better person. If they hadn't, I'd probably still be the dick that I was in my early twenties. Not only did Rel tell me, truthfully, that he didn't like the person I'd become, but my parents also sat me down and gave me a talking-to. Instead of helping me out in the situation with Mark, they made me pay for Mark's hospital bills and surgery—at a cost of thousands of dollars. And then they told me that it was time for me to stop fucking up, and that if I did screw up again, they weren't going to bail me out.

I am thrilled that they did that. For the first time, I began to think about the repercussions of my actions. Instead of thinking "I want it, so I'm going to do it" the way I always had, I began to consider the fact that everything I did reflected on my family and friends. My parents' brutal honesty opened my eyes to the way my behavior affected the people I loved and admired.

If you ever plan on evolving as a person, you need to surround yourself with people who will point out your flaws and aggressively challenge you to improve yourself. Sure, you can also challenge yourself, as I did, but I was always inspired first by the honesty of my friends. You can't expect to grow or change if you choose friends who aren't willing to criticize you.

Often, we try to become friends with people who are similar to us—*too* similar. They'll share the same interests, the same jokes, and the same habits. As a result, they won't inspire us to grow. Often I notice that lazy people hang out with other lazy people, playing videogames and smoking pot, instead of hanging out with that friend who is really hustling to get a business started. Jocks hang out with jocks, type A's with type A's, the paranoid with other paranoid types, all of us feeding one another's habits and dysfunctions. After all, for someone struggling with their weight, the less painful choice is to hang out with the friend who can commiserate over food and the number on the scale rather than the friend who eats her kale salads and works out. We don't want to hear the hard truth about the mistakes we are making, so instead, we surround ourselves with people who are making the same mistakes.

Everyone needs a friend who tells them the hard truth. And not just when they mess up, either. As you go through life you're constantly going to run into situations that are difficult and confusing and emotional. An honest opinion and some heartfelt advice from a close friend is the foundation of every good decision. (I bet that at least half of the catfish victims I've met shooting our TV show would have ended their online relationships sooner if a friend had just sat them down and given them some tough love.) When you're looking for friends, seek out people who will be honest with you and whom you can be honest with, too.

To this day, Rel and Henry remain my closest friends and collaborators, the people who tell me what I really need to hear. My parents have never had to bail me out again. And I've made new friends, too; people who inspire me and who aren't afraid of really giving it to me when I deserve it—like Max, who recently called me out when I was being unintentionally insensitive to the hardworking crew on my show. He was totally right, and thanks to him, I went to work on improving my behavior. (Even now, eight years after the incident with Mark, I'm still working on becoming a better person. It's a never-ending process.)

And I'm also happy to say that my friendship with Mark—though maybe not what it perhaps could have been—is really strong again. For my last birthday, he sent me a short text: "Happy Birthday Penis." Believe me when I say that, coming from Mark, this is a term of affection.

CHAPTER 17

How to Apologize

I come from a long line of practical jokers and goofballs. Just one example: My grandfather Marvin used to think it was funny when women put on lipstick at the table after the meal was over. So one night, after dinner at a restaurant, when the wives all pulled out their compacts to touch up their makeup, he whipped out his electric razor and started buzzing his beard right there at the table.

My uncle Michael is cut from the same cloth. Sit near him at a restaurant and at any moment you might expect a bread roll to come whizzing by your head. Once, at a fancy fundraiser, he thought it would be funny to slip the expensive silverware into the purse of the woman sitting next to him—who happened to be of some royal European descent—and pretend she'd stolen it. Unfortunately, the forks and knives had already been used, and they ruined her incredibly expensive silk purse. She was not amused.

When I was growing up, Michael's wife—my aunt Candy—was constantly scolding him about his antics. And yet she always seemed to forgive him. No matter how badly he screwed up, it didn't seem to negatively affect their marriage. I always wondered: How did he get away with it?

Finally, when I was twelve, I asked him. The secret to his ability to get away with murder? "Never forget these words: 'I'm sorry. I was wrong,' " he told me. "It's just five words, and they will end an argument every time. Especially an argument with a woman. It doesn't matter what you're fighting about, or even if you know you're right. If you want to release the tension and move forward, just say it. 'I'm sorry. I was wrong.' "

I took his advice to heart and began a long and illustrious career as a profligate apologizer.

I had a lot to apologize for. I got in a tremendous amount of trouble. I was constantly making mistakes. After my uncle clued me in to his secret, I began apologizing constantly. It was my automatic response to any mistake I made, my get-out-of-jail-free card. *I guess I did something wrong because you're unhappy and I'm in trouble, so "I'm sorry!" Now we're all square, right? I said what I'm supposed to say, and that's it!*

I soon mastered the art of the apology: how to articulately state what I'd done wrong, say that I was sorry, and convince whoever was mad at me that I'd learned my lesson and felt really terrible about it. I apologized to my friends, my teachers, my family—even the police, when I had to. I could convince almost anyone that I was sorry and that I wouldn't do it again…right up until the moment that I *would* do it again. I'd play the part of the repentant screwup until the curtain dropped, and then I'd be right back at it. It was as if I had my fingers perpetually crossed behind my back.

I was the most disingenuous person I knew: I wasn't really sorry, I didn't really regret it, and my remorse was totally false.

For a long time, my uncle's advice seemed to work. Until finally, during one of the most critical moments in my life—when I punched my best friend in the face—it didn't.

Mark was in the hospital with his skull cracked open. It was totally my fault. Everyone was upset with me. So I whipped out my usual apologies and dispensed one to everyone involved. *I'm sorry, I was wrong. I'm sorry, I was wrong. I'm sorry, I was wrong!*

For once I really was sorry, but this time, instead of forgiving me, Mark stopped speaking to me altogether. My parents didn't buy my apology. My brother didn't want to be my friend anymore. I was like the boy who cried wolf: I'd screwed up so much without changing my behavior that no one actually believed my contrition anymore. I couldn't apologize my way out of this situation, because everyone knew that my apologies were meaningless.

That's when it struck me that I'd been writing bad apology checks for years, and now they were bouncing. My apology credit with my family had run out. I was broke. My words had no value.

At that moment I realized that I couldn't just *say* I was sorry—I had to actually *be* sorry. I had to *demonstrate* how sorry I was and make sure that it would never happen again. A true apology in that situation could never be expressed in words, no matter how well-crafted. It had to be an emotional, sincere, and observable change in behavior.

There's an implied commitment when you apologize for something: a promise that you won't do it again. My uncle's advice was only half of the story. Saying "I'm sorry" *isn't* a get-out-of-jail-free card. It's just the first step toward making a change.

But a real, genuine apology *can* be incredibly effective. People are afraid to admit when they are wrong and take that hit, but the ability to confess your mistakes and take steps to address your behavior is at the foundation of all real relationships.

These days, I take my apologies really seriously. When someone (say, my girlfriend) is upset with me, I don't just immediately say "I'm sorry." (Except for farts. Apologies for farts should be instantaneous.) Instead, I take a minute—sometimes ten, a couple of hours at the most. I *think* about what the person is upset about and really consider my behavior. And only then do I go back and apologize. It takes longer, but it's done with real consideration, meaning, and self-reflection.

And then, most importantly, I try to figure out how I can change my behavior to ensure that I won't screw up in the same way again.

That's not to say that it's gotten easy for me—it's a constant process of evolution. For example, at the end of shooting season 2 of *Catfish*, I found myself in Pensacola, Florida, with the rest of the production team, shooting the Mike and Heather/Caroline episode (episode 215). It was day two of the episode—our "investigation day." On the show, this looks like a fun process, full of twists and turns. But that's because you're only seeing four minutes of what's usually an eight-hour process. The other seven hours and fifty-six minutes we're doing painstaking, frustrating, and often completely fruitless Internet research.

This is hands down my least favorite day of the episode. On that day in Pensacola, I was particularly irritable. It was the end of the summer. We'd been shooting for five months. And I was cranky. A few hours into the investigation, we finally made a discovery: One photo of our catfish, "Caroline," turned out to have been geotagged. A "pin" on the photo showed us an apartment complex in Pensacola, a big two-story building with dozens of units.

Max immediately got excited: "Oh my God, the pin falls right on unit two-twenty-three! Let's go investigate that apartment!" But I blew off his excitement, saying, "Max, the pin is just a triangulated position within a hundred yards of that spot. There are forty apartments within that pin drop. It's a dead end." It turned into a heated discussion, escalating to the point where I told Max that he was being dumb and wasting our time. In those exact words.

Max shrugged and walked out of the room. Meanwhile, in front of the entire crew, I threw my iPhone in a fit of rage, shattering it.

A few minutes later, Max came back into the room and said, "Nev, sometimes you can be a real dick. You need to be more careful about the way you talk to people. You need *all of us* to make this show. If you're speaking down to us, we aren't going to want to work with you. You gotta get this under control. You're hurting people's feelings."

At first I was furious that he'd said this in front of the whole crew. But then I realized that he was dead on. "You're right," I said. "I'm sorry. You guys are like my family on the road. I take our friendships for granted because we work together." And I vowed that from that point on, I'd make sure that no matter who I was talking to, I'd try to be as kind and respectful and humble and pleasant as I could be.

It's hard, and I'm still working on it. But Max's confrontation was a turning point for me, a moment of honesty and self-realization that changed me. This was only a year ago, but I've taken significant actions as a result. Now I try to look at every email I write before I send it. I think about what I'm going to say before I say it. I make sure I'm employing the most constructive words to get my message across.

That was a real apology—one that resulted in me working on myself and showing through my actions that I'm going to change.

———

If you watch *Catfish*, you know that we hear a lot of apologies on the show. Almost every episode ends with one person—sometimes both—apologizing for the lies they've told. My experience with what happens *next* is proof that saying "I'm sorry" is only the first step in repairing your relationship.

The ugly truth of our show is that our hopefuls rarely forgive and forget. And why should they? This catfish that they've been communicating with for months or years has lied to them! Just saying "I'm sorry" isn't going to cut it, no matter how much the catfish professes their remorse. After all, if the catfish truly understood that what they did was wrong, why didn't they apologize sooner? Instead, for their entire relationship, they chose to hurt, deceive, and betray the trust of the person they supposedly cared for. So even though they are admitting that what they did was wrong, that isn't going to absolve them of their sins.

Instead, an apology from the catfish is just the first step. What needs to happen next? A total restart. They need to build a whole new relationship that's filled *only* with actions that express how contrite they are. Only once the catfish has reintroduced honesty and trust into a relationship can it reboot and grow again. After that, anything can happen.

The majority of the relationships we investigate and expose on *Catfish* never get past that initial "I'm sorry." The catfish apologizes, but the apology is empty. Nothing changes. The relationship is over for good. The catfish goes back to their life as it was before; maybe they even go back to catfishing.

Every once in a while, though, we expose a catfish who uses their apology as the jumping-off point for a whole new way of existence. And these moments can be truly inspiring.

Chelsea was a teenage girl who, for years, had been pretending to be a man online (episode 101). Using the fake Facebook profile of a male model named Jamison, she cultivated an online romance with a girl named Sunny. When we exposed her on the first season of the show, Chelsea wasn't apologetic at first. Only after we broke down her protective wall did she apologize. Sunny even accepted her apology. There was talk about the two remaining friends, and at first they did, but it fizzled out quickly. The trust just wasn't there.

But Chelsea took her apology seriously, and she went on to turn her experience into a real, positive, life-changing moment. She decided that she was finished with pretending to be someone she wasn't on the Internet. Instead, she embraced who she really was, and came out to her community as a lesbian. And then she started an online support group, helping other people like her. She now runs a Twitter support page. She's constantly fielding emails and phone calls from other teenagers who are confused about their sexuality and playing with false identities; she's become a real source of strength.

In her case, an apology *was* the starting point, rather than an end goal.

———

A lot of people avoid apologies altogether. It's easier to pretend you didn't do anything wrong than it is to apologize and have to address your mistakes. But the truth is that an apology can be incredibly cathartic. It's a chance to start fresh, even to become a better person. It is, in other words, a really great opportunity—even if it doesn't feel that way.

We're all familiar with that awkward, uncomfortable moment when you're in the room with someone you've hurt and you *know* you need to break the ice and apologize. Whether your parents are upset because you broke something or your girlfriend found out that you cheated on her, broaching that conversation can be really tough. But when you do, it's a relief to finally have it out on the table, rather than eating you up on the inside. Once it's out, it can be addressed, and only then can it be *resolved*.

But some people just won't do it. They let it linger. Tension builds. And relationships get really toxic because there's something festering, invisibly, that everyone is trying to ignore. I constantly meet people who aren't talking to their siblings or their best friends because they got in a fight and neither was willing to apologize. A day or two becomes a week. A month. Years go by. And what could have been resolved easily with an apology from both sides instead leads to a lifetime of bitterness and regret.

It may seem counterintuitive, but the fastest way to feel better is to be accountable and take responsibility for your mistake. It's like washing dishes—the longer you put it off, the more it sucks. Those dishes are never going to go away. They just get grosser and grosser, piling up higher and higher until you deal with them. But if you address them right away? The work is fairly painless. Your kitchen is clean, and you feel great.

Here's an example: My freshman year of college, I discovered a four-room storage basement in my dorm that the maintenance men had forgotten to lock up. I quickly appropriated two of the rooms as a party pad. I cleaned them up and dragged in a sound system, a minifridge, furniture, and fans. I decked the space out. And then I threw parties for all my dormmates and friends.

I totally got away with it, too, until the maintenance men came back and discovered my lava lamps and sound system. They locked the basement and put up a sign that read THE PROPERTY IN THE BASEMENT HAS BEEN CONFISCATED. Everyone in my dorm began to freak out: *What should we do? What if we get in trouble?* My friends began to worry about getting thrown out of the dorm.

I decided to curb the rising drama by going to confess. I walked up to the administration building, knocked on the door of the student activities director, and, to his surprise, said, "Look, I'm sorry about what happened. I know I shouldn't have done it. But can I get my stuff back?"

It's true that at this point in my life, I was handing out apologies left and right without changing my actions. Still, I took responsibility for what I'd done instead of hiding, even if I was not yet mature enough to follow through with changing the behavior that led to the apology.

It wasn't as if I skated off without punishment: I got put on housing probation. Still, it could have been a lot worse. By taking responsibility and apologizing, I quashed the whole issue. The drama blew over within a day or two, rather than escalating into a finger-pointing session that might have ended my friendship with my dormmates. Who knows, people might even have been expelled. Instead, my dormmates were relieved that I'd taken the fall, and we all moved on. It was cathartic for everyone.

I even got my stuff back.

Human instinct is always to avoid drama. But raising your hand when you are responsible, and raising it right away, is *always* the best way to deal with an issue. Because the problem isn't going to go away on its own. Even if you are able to operate "as usual," an unresolved issue will continue to weigh on you and the person you've affected. Once you've stepped up, taken responsibility, and apologized, not only can you start figuring out how to fix your problem, but you've also taken away the reason for the other person to be upset with you. Which, in turn, allows for healing the relationship.

So in a way, my uncle Mike was right after all. When used appropriately and sincerely, an apology is the best move you can make. It puts you on higher ground. It's a surefire way to feel better. Even though it might lead to a difficult emotional conversation that you'd rather avoid, an apology is always the start of a better life.

The sooner you learn to do it, the sooner you get to the good stuff.

CHAPTER 18

On New Year's Day of 2012, I woke up with the blinding sunshine of a Florida morning streaming straight into my face. Where was I? Oh yeah: the guest bedroom of my father's condo in West Palm Beach. My temples throbbed; my tongue tasted of sour alcohol; my body odor was beastly. I could feel a wicked hangover coming on. And—oh crap—I wasn't alone.

Next to me was a girl. I knew her name (well, I knew her first name, at least) but barely anything else about her. She looked as rough as I felt—her mascara smeared, her face puffy with exhaustion and booze. There was some kind of crusty infection in one of her eyes. Pinkeye? As I looked at it, I could feel my own eye starting to itch. Served me right.

My memories of the previous evening were hazy. There had been a nightclub and too much alcohol. I remembered hopping in a taxi to my dad's place with this girl in tow, and I also remembered having drunken, passionless, downright awful sex. So bad that neither of us had even finished what we'd started: Thanks to the amount of alcohol in my system, I wasn't exactly fully operational.

Looking at the girl asleep next to me—someone I didn't care about and wasn't even particularly attracted to—I felt gross. *This isn't working,* I thought to myself. *I'm never going to find the love of my life by picking up girls and having meaningless sex with them. Something needs to change.*

It may sound extreme, but in a moment of clarity, I knew exactly what I needed to do: I had to write off sex. It would be my New Year's resolution! *A vow of celibacy.* I liked the way it sounded. I felt *relieved.* It was simple: I would avoid all sexual contact for a year. No sex. No kissing. No flirting. No nothing.

It's not like I'd been a total man-whore, but I wasn't exactly a saint, either. To put it delicately, I'd had enough sex to feel compelled to make a list with the names of all the girls I'd done it with, so that my sexual partners didn't just become an accruing number. It seemed like a good idea: I wanted to remember who those girls were and where I was at the time. Maybe that in itself was a sign that I'd had sex with a few women too many.

But that was only part of the problem.

I was a notorious flirt, and had been since I was eight or nine years old. I'd always had confidence beyond my years. I'd taken to heart my dad's advice about women: "Just tell them what you think of them. Women love being told that you think they're beautiful." I had no shame about approaching women. If a woman was even remotely attractive to me, I would flatter and flirt—to the point where women would often feel uncomfortable.

By the time I was in my twenties, my sexuality was out of control. I cheated on my girlfriends. I flirted with friends' girlfriends. I had one-night stands.

And then there were the women on Facebook.

I had categorized a special group called "Cute Girls" on Facebook—my digital "little black book"—and I would browse these profiles on a regular basis. When I met women, in real life or online, I'd file them away in that Facebook group and then I would chat with them, text with them, conduct distracting Twitter flirtations. I wasn't actually dating all of them at once (most of them I never even saw in real life), but I liked the idea of always having a number of girls on the hook. After all, my dad had always encouraged me to be assertive and outgoing, to approach ten girls in order to get two phone numbers. "Enough to keep you busy," he'd say.

I loved the high of pursuing someone. The challenge of figuring out what to say. The hunt. The conquest. I made the pursuit of women a part-time job in order to justify how much time I spent on it. (And to justify the amount of time I *didn't* spend doing other, more productive things. Like working.) I pretended I was looking for a girlfriend; and sure, maybe I was. But I was going about it all wrong. It was like pulling a slot machine trying to win the jackpot. It just doesn't work. You might get a couple coins back and feel like you're getting closer, but you're not.

My relationship with Megan epitomized all of this. It was

surface, fun, seemingly intimate but ultimately shallow. It felt exciting, and sure, I had told her some secrets, but the relationship wasn't based on anything real or honest.

You'd think that experience would have taught me an immediate lesson. It didn't. Instead, as the *Catfish* documentary came out and my new notoriety helped me meet more women, I became even more cavalier. I broke up with Katie, my long-term girlfriend, because I thought I should be single and free (a decision I ended up regretting). I'd make dates with women and then skip out on them the minute I found something or someone more interesting to do. I was *that guy*—the unpredictable, selfish bachelor dude. (Trust me: You're glad you weren't dating me.)

By the time New Year's 2012 rolled around, my behavior was at its worst. And when I woke up that morning, hungover, with an itchy eye and a deep sense of shame, I knew it was the moment to find a new way. I was about to start working on *Catfish: The TV Show*, and I needed to focus all my energy on that opportunity. I wanted to clean up my act, eliminate the distractions in my life.

A vow of celibacy just made sense. It would be the cleanse I needed.

My friends were in shock when I told them. A group of them even put together a betting pool: two thousand dollars said I wouldn't make it the full year. I laughed along with them, but I knew that it wasn't just about keeping it in my pants for 365 days. It was about changing my behavior so that I was no longer interacting with women on a sexual level only. Instead, I would talk to them, listen to them, have (gasp!) meaningful conversations. I didn't ever want to have empty sex again.

I deleted my "Cute Girl" group on Facebook, and then, not long afterward, deleted my Facebook account entirely.

At first it was hard, but a month into the experiment, I started feeling really good. And then I started feeling great. I actually felt more confident about myself now that I didn't need a woman's attention to boost my ego. I enjoyed surprising women by *not* flirting with them—and it turned out that being the guy who *didn't* hit on them just made me more interesting. (Bonus! More women interested in me! Too bad I couldn't take them up on it.) Being in control of my sexuality felt awesome, and people noticed it. They were surprised at and delighted by my new energy, and that made me feel even better about myself.

You could argue that I also got a kind of thrill out of trying not to be sexual with the women I met. Maybe that's true. But—if I were to make an analogy—it was the difference between the way a lion hunts to catch and devour its prey and the way a squirrel collects and stores nuts for winter. I understood that I was investing in a longer-term, more sustainable satisfaction rather than a quick rush.

I was finally learning how to be comfortable alone. Nights when I went home by myself—nights when I normally would have felt lonely and texted a Cute Girl—I was now happy just watching a movie and going to bed. Being by myself was more satisfying than the inevitably empty exchange of casual sex, I realized. For the first time, I started to really like myself.

And that's when I finally found love.

Shanee was a woman I'd been dating on and off since the summer of 2011; a cool indie musician with a face straight out of a Botticelli painting. At first, I'd treated her awfully. As she'd told me during a quarrel not long after we started dating, "You are a selfish and self-centered guy who doesn't know what you want and pretends to be happy but deep down is really just afraid and lonely." She had me pegged, but I wasn't ready to hear it yet, so our relationship stalled after just a few months. Still, her words stuck with me, and after I took my vow of celibacy, I decided to make an effort to really build a friendship with her. Best decision ever.

Our friendship began to grow. I respected how she challenged me about what I was doing, forced me to answer hard questions about myself, and helped me realize that my aggressive sexuality was just a way to distract myself from my loneliness and fear. During my conversations with Shanee, I started to see that I'd never felt the connection to my girlfriends that I was capable of. I'd been using my "joie de Nev-re" to keep things very surface-level. I'd filled my life with things that were fun and appealing to girls—I had a motorcycle, access to my dad's weekend home in the Hamptons, a big social circle—but I didn't actually open up to anyone, online or off. I was never honest with myself and as a result couldn't be honest with them.

But I was being honest and vulnerable with *her*, for the first time in my life. We had a few more false starts, but by the summer of 2012 I began to feel real love for Shanee. And that's when my vow of celibacy started to get hard. Really hard. We would snuggle and take naps together, but believe me: It's not the same thing. Although Shanee supported my celibacy, she thought it was crazy to deny myself. "Why are you really doing this?" she would ask me. "It's not to see if you can go a whole year. That's stupid. If the point is to feel love, then when you feel that, you're done."

She was right. And so after 265 days, we made love. It was long enough.

(For those of you who bet against me, feel free to send me a PayPal invoice.)

———

I learned a lot of things during those 265 days of celibacy—including how much money I could save when I wasn't trying to seduce girls with overpriced cocktails at pretentious mixology bars—but the most important lesson was this: Being ready to love is all about tapping into the power of vulnerability.

Loving somebody isn't just about saying the right things, or just "being there." In order to really show someone that you love them, and to let them love you, you need to be vulnerable and open. That's scary. Often it means admitting that you don't know something, that you're upset and confused and afraid. It means exposing your weaknesses. Admitting when you're wrong. Allowing yourself to trust someone else with your most sensitive, deepest, darkest feelings.

Social media can get in the way of all this. Facebook and Twitter present a very unrealistic playing field where people are meant to interact and share but are never expected to actually conduct a meaningful exchange. It's easy to go on Facebook and present ourselves in a way that we think people will like. To be the best version of ourselves. In my case it was, *"Hey, I'm Nev! I'm this confident guy with a fun life!"* I never thought it would be in my best interest to expose the fact that I was confused and felt lost a lot of the time and was unhappy with who I was. Who wanted to hear *that*?

Instead, I presented a facade and absorbed "affection" from all those Cute Girls—but it caused more harm than good. It distracted me from what's real.

Here's the thing: You can *control* your Internet profile. You turn it on and off, you choose what to say and delete, and when you are uncomfortable you can log out. Real relationships aren't like that. By being so invested in our "easy" online selves, we often avoid taking the time to understand our more challenging actual selves.

Remember your blankie from when you were a kid? Your mom probably still has it in a closet somewhere. It's gross, and it smells, and when you look at it now you realize how flimsy and insubstantial it is. But back then, it was everything: the friend that kept you safe from monsters in the dark, from scary situations, from feeling vulnerable. It was a crutch.

It's not so adorable when you're dragging around that bedraggled blanket as a twenty- or thirty-year-old, though. So instead, as adults, what do we use? We're still afraid of being vulnerable—especially in love—so we've found a new crutch in the Internet. Another world, full of "friends" that make us feel safe. But social media is kind of like that stinky blanket: an inanimate object that doesn't give us real emotion or affection. Maybe it makes us feel less vulnerable, but that's only because it's distracting us from the important stuff. It's the grown-up equivalent of pulling a blanket over our head in the dark.

Connections and friendships can take all forms, and social media can be an excellent way to meet someone, but the truth is you're never going to have a meaningful relationship if you aren't willing to take it beyond the digital realm and be vulnerable in front of a real, live person. Social media provides the illusion of intimacy, but it doesn't deliver the real thing. If your digital friendships are replacing your real-life friendships—and if your profile persona is replacing your real-life personality—it's time to have some real talk with yourself about whether or not you are doing the work that will bring you real satisfaction.

With "Megan," I was in love with a Facebook profile; an idea; a voice on the phone. I was never really open and vulnerable with her; and so I was never really in love with her, even though I believed I was. Phones and computers are a filter, and there's no filter in real life; I never had to expose myself to her in an honest, face-to-face environment with a real risk of judgment. In the end, neither "Megan" nor I had any clue who the other person was.

It took disconnecting from the Internet and going out into the real world—disengaging from the fun online persona and really working hard to be more vulnerable—for me to find real love.

> The rise of online-only relationships [has created] a phenomenon I've begun to call Soul Mate in a Box. A Soul Mate in a Box (Smiab, for short) is a person we rarely if ever meet and in some cases never speak to, but to whom we feel closer than anyone else.... We're always searching for new ways of finding love that don't involve having to feel insecure and vulnerable...and we're fooled into thinking this may be a better and truer way of having a relationship.
>
> —Daniel Jones, editor of the *New York Times* Modern Love column, in the *New York Times*

———

This is a book about friending yourself. If you are still reading (as opposed to Instagramming photos of your cat), it's because you are curious about how to better understand and live a life that is real, honest, and fulfilling. And sure, we need to be real and honest in the ways that we interact online—but we also need to be real and honest with *ourselves*.

What does it mean to be realistic with yourself? Sometimes it means taking ownership of your problems and saying, "This sucks, I'm bad at that, I don't like who I'm being right now." Or "I'm unhappy, what am I doing wrong, how can I fix it?" We need to stop pretending to be happy online and figure out how to *really* be happy.

Casey Neistat made a great short film about being a frequent flier on American Airlines. He flies so often that he gets treated like a king, gets tons of perks, and almost never pays for a flight anymore. He says that airlines are like women: None of them are perfect, but when you commit to one of them, that's when you start to see the rewards.

I know that *I'm* not perfect. And that there's no perfect girl. No perfect guy. No perfect couple. There are just people who are willing to try—to accept and compromise and see through the superficial to what really counts. It's never going to be easy. Any real relationship has issues and speed bumps. But the only way you'll be able to achieve a meaningful connection is if you're willing to commit and put in the work—with your partner and with yourself.

My celibacy vow started with a commitment to not be sexual, and right away that felt good. And then it was a commitment to be more communicative, and that felt great. And then it was a commitment to try to understand what I was doing and what my actions actually meant. And that was tremendous. I learned that the unbelievable satisfaction and excitement that come from just choosing to commit—from giving everything I have—is one of the best feelings in the world.

Everything starts with a decision, a simple moment: Am I going to do this? Yes or no? The only way to change and learn, to discover who you really are and be happy, is to go for it.

So what did I learn from my nine months of celibacy? That being ready to love has nothing to do with anybody else and everything to do with yourself.

> *Your task is not to seek for love, but merely to seek and find all the barriers within yourself that you have built against it.*
>
> —widely attributed to Rumi, Sufi poet

CHAPTER 19

Relationships and Self-Esteem

Hi. My name's Nev. And I'm a jerk.

Actually, it's fairer to say that I *used* to be a jerk. Specifically, I was a jerk to women. Even more specifically, I was a jerk to my (now) girlfriend, Shanee. When I met Shanee, in the summer of 2011, I behaved like one of *those guys*—the kind of guy you tell your friend she should dump because he just isn't treating her the way she deserves to be treated.

Shanee deserved a lot more from me than I gave her, but I didn't realize that at first. Instead, I was totally inconsiderate. I dated other women. I'd talk about how cute other girls were right in front of her. I'd text her instead of calling her. I'd make plans and then cancel them. We lost touch for a long time, for good reason. And then, after I took my celibacy vow and reached out to Shanee again, I told her that I wanted to be "just friends"—and yet every time we were together, I would try to kiss her neck or hold her hand.

My reservations about being in a relationship with Shanee were petty, at best. I had decided right off the bat that she was not my dream girl. She wasn't my physical type, to start: Having been in a three-year relationship with a professional ballerina, I was used to women who were outrageously toned and lean. Shanee had a more feminine figure. And she was an indie musician whose music I wasn't particularly moved by at the time. (I've since come to love her music!)

Tactful me, I actually told her this. "What you do doesn't excite me. It doesn't turn me on," I said one day, not long after we reconnected post–chastity vow.

But her response to this surprised me. Instead of getting pissed off or hurt or equivocal, Shanee made her determination perfectly clear. "Well, listen, I don't care what you think," she said. "I chose to follow my heart's desire even though it's not practical or profitable. I believe I will succeed because I have something to say."

At that moment, I began to seriously respect her. She had held her own against my criticism without backing down. Not only that, but she soon began to draw the line when it came to my completely unacceptable behavior. "You can't tell me you're going to meet with me and cancel at the last minute," she informed me. "You can't talk about cute girls in front of me. And I want you to talk to me on the phone instead of just texting me all the time—that kind of communication isn't real."

Every time Shanee challenged or confronted me, it separated her from all the other women I had dated. She was elevated, in my eyes, because of her confidence and self-respect. The more she drew the line with me, the more my interest in her grew.

Finally, she gave me an ultimatum. "What are you *doing*?" she said one night when I was attempting to kiss her neck again (yeah, it was getting harder and harder for me to maintain my chastity vow). "Look—I'd love to be your *friend*, but that's not what's going on here. I have feelings for you. If you acknowledge that I'm your girlfriend, and that this is how we're behaving, we can hang out again. Until then, I'm not going to spend time with you, because you're not respecting my needs."

For a few months after she laid down the law, we didn't speak. And I missed her terribly. I began to realize how important she was in my life; how much I wanted her in it. I reached out to her again. "I don't have many friends," I told her. "Our relationship means so much to me; please stay in my life and forgive me for being an asshole."

Maybe I wouldn't have chosen Shanee out of a potential-girlfriend lineup before, but I was starting to realize that what was inside her mattered far more than any idealized fictional girl. She *was* beautiful, of course. But the sexiest thing in the world is confidence, and Shanee was fully aware of who she was and *happy* about it. Not only that, she had the self-esteem to not let me walk all over her.

"We love each other for who we are, and it doesn't matter what we really look like, because love is on the inside." I've heard this line so many times from catfish on the show, but it's not true—at least not in that *Beauty and the Beast* Disneyfied way. Looks *do* matter when it comes to physical attraction. *But*—and this is a big *but*—if you're really serious about being in a relationship, your preconceived notion about how your partner should look doesn't matter quite as much as you think it does. Remember earlier in the book when I said that physical attraction is key to romantic relationships? This is the other side of that. A chemical reaction between two people is essential—but it can come in an unexpected form. Sometimes one person's attraction to another has more to do with what that person projects to the world than it does with any specific physical attributes.

What matters most? Self-respect. Confidence. Strength.

Shanee's confidence was attractive to me: It was what I wanted in myself. And her self-respect was what ultimately caused me to fall in love with her.

———

When you take a look at my mom, it makes sense that I was drawn to Shanee's confidence. My mom is also an incredibly strong, self-assured woman, and her positive influence on me has resonated through every relationship I've ever had with a woman.

My mom's confidence and belief in herself is blatantly obvious in everything she does—from riding a motorcycle to getting tattoos (she has lots), from her lifelong love of art to the eclectic way she decorates her home. She's gone back to school twice as an adult: once for a continuing education course in film production at NYU, and again, at age fifty-five, for a masters in social work. She's gone through several careers, and now she runs a chapter of the terrific nonprofit Leave Out Violence, which is working to end the cycle of violence youth to youth.

I never knew my mom when she was a teenager (obviously) but from what she tells me, her sense of self was severely tested when she was in high school. She was diagnosed with scoliosis at age fifteen and had to have her spine fused, top to bottom. The doctors made her wear a full back brace—you know, the Elizabethan collar that you see in movies about nerd kids? Yeah, that. *Shudder.* Before the brace, she had been a ballerina; after the brace, she was an outcast. But she kept her head down, focused on getting out of there, and made it to a great liberal arts college—even with people sticking magnets on her brace in the high school hallways.

By her early twenties, she was married with two kids (yes, I'm referring to Rel and myself). She wasn't happy, though. So, at age twenty-six, she decided to leave my dad and raise her kids as a single mom. It was a courageous move to leave behind the security of marriage, going against both societal pressures and the urgings of her mother.

Her clarity about what she wanted worked in her favor. Within a few years, she'd met the man who would be my stepfather, Sheldon. Once again, she set a high bar for herself: He was still technically married at the time, and she told him that she wouldn't date him until he was officially divorced: "I don't want to be a part of your issues," she told him.

So he got divorced in order to date her. And then, when he wanted her to marry him, she made him ask her a half dozen times before she said yes.

My mom knew what she wanted from life and wasn't afraid to set boundaries for herself. She didn't worry too much about what the people around her would think. I'd be lying if I said that my mom didn't care *at all* about what people thought about her. But she didn't let that get in the way of pursuing the things she wanted. She wasn't afraid to try things. She had a very strong sense of who she was. Her self-respect was—and still is—apparent to everyone around her.

It's not a great time to be dating. We "hook up" instead of going out. We text and text without ever really speaking. We don't make plans until the very last minute, because it's so easy to avoid the commitment of setting a time and place.

Meanwhile, we bend over backward in order to be loved. Instead of saying, "This is who I am and if you don't like it, fine," we pretend to be things that we aren't. We lower our standards. Both men and women do this, but I've witnessed a lot of women in particular sell themselves short. They buy into the Hollywood stereotype of being passive and waiting for Mr. Wonderful to sweep them off their feet. They start changing their priorities in order to be with a guy they really like. They worry more about pleasing the person they're dating than about pleasing themselves.

I'm sure you have a friend who does this. A girl who puts up with a guy who texts her at 2 a.m. for booty calls but ignores her the rest of the week. A girl who pretends that she's fine spending her "one-on-one time" with her boyfriend, watching him and his friends play videogames—because she is afraid to insist on going out, just the two of them. A girl who acts as if it's totally fine that the guy she is dating is never nice to her in public, because she secretly believes this negative attention is better than no attention at all.

As a man, let me tell you: Men aren't attracted to this kind of self-effacing behavior. In fact, it's the opposite. When you hold your own and know yourself, when you recognize what's important to you and are faithful to that above all else, *that's* when real men take you seriously as a human being. When you respect yourself, the world will respect you back. *You* set the stage for how you want people to treat you.

For generations, women have been conditioned to be adaptable to the men that they are with. Men have been conditioned to be the opposite—to be the leaders. But times are changing; the world is waking up. Roles have shifted a little. Men are more like the stereotype of "women," and women are more like "men." This is a great time for women to hone their sense of self, and find a real partner who loves them for who they are.

Far too many people are looking for the right person,
instead of trying to be the right person.
—Gloria Steinem, feminist activist

Unfortunately, the age of social media is making that shift harder than it should be. Instead of being forthright with the people we are dating, we try to glean clues from their Twitter posts and relationship status updates. We communicate via texts instead of phone calls. We spend our time together on Gchat and Facebook instead of going out on actual dates. A relationship that's based primarily on digital communication is not one that's rooted in confidence and self-esteem. It's about hedging around commitment, keeping your options open, and avoiding the hard realities of dating.

The culture of commitment-free digital communication may make it more difficult than ever to assert yourself, but confidence and self-esteem will always break through the noise. After all, if a guy balks when you ask him to call instead of text, is that really a guy you want to be with in the long term? Only when you raise your standards, assert your needs, and get your relationship offline will you finally find real love.

———

You can't rely on someone else to feel good about yourself. If you judge your worth based on the person you are dating or the people you are friends with, you will never be happy.

Love isn't the answer, either. Growing up, we're led to believe that love is a fairy tale. Love solves everything: Find it, and you're set for life. We believe in love at first sight, and that once you meet that perfectly fitting "soul mate" the rest is easy. There's no need to work on yourself, because the person you've found will love you unconditionally.

That couldn't be farther from the truth. In reality, relationships require constant care and maintenance. And you as an individual have to challenge yourself to grow and improve so you can bring that self-knowledge to your relationship. The only way to keep things interesting is to keep challenging each other.

Love alone cannot sustain a meaningful relationship. Rather, the most important part of a relationship is communication. You need to be able to have a really good, open dialogue with the other person. (Same goes for your friends!) Be honest, and be willing to address issues as they come up. Because there are *always* issues.

My relationship with Shanee was the opposite of the fairy tale. It was not love at first sight; things grew slowly, and making our relationship work was hard. And still is! But I've learned that things don't need to be perfect. There just needs to be a connection. There needs to be a willingness to do the work a relationship takes. And there needs to be confidence that you can get it done without losing yourself in the bargain.

CHAPTER 20

You Only Regret the Things You Don't Do

My friend Casey Neistat was born in New London, Connecticut, to a lower-income family. Like me, he was a trouble-maker when he was young. At age fifteen, he got his girlfriend pregnant. By the time he was sixteen, he was already a dad. He dropped out of high school in order to work, and got a dead-end job washing dishes at a local diner. He lived in a trailer park with his son and his son's mother. He was on welfare to make ends meet.

That could easily have been the end of his story right there—going nowhere fast.

But that's not what Casey wanted from life. He had drive. His older brother Van had graduated from college, moved to New York City, and found a job as a studio assistant for an artist named Tom Sachs. When Casey heard about what Van was doing, he thought, "I can do that." So he drove to New York City, lied to Tom Sachs about his experience, and got a job as an office assistant—cleaning, organizing, and making more than he'd been making as a dishwasher. He was now surrounded by really interesting people who inspired him; meanwhile, he was also committed to helping raise his son, and went back to Connecticut every weekend to spend time with him. It was hard, but he found a way.

In not much time at all, Casey and Van had saved up enough money to buy an early iMac—the first computer you could edit video on. They maxed out their credit cards, bought a video camera, and started making short films. The first film they made was a rant about the iPod—one of their favorite toys—and how the battery was irreplaceable (when you called Apple to complain about the short battery life, they simply told you to buy a new one). Casey and Van put their film online, and it became (arguably) the first viral video ever, with millions of views.

Soon, Apple was changing its battery exchange policy. And the phenomenon of the Neistat brothers was born. As a team, they posted more short films online—sixty-seven at last count. HBO gave them a TV series. They produced two feature-length films.

Nothing Casey did with his life was conventional. He followed none of the predetermined paths toward success in commercial filmmaking. Instead, he blazed a new path with nothing more than willpower. He wasn't born with any advantages. He's not a typically good-looking guy (he'll be the first to tell you that), but he's very attractive to women because he's creative and confident. He believes in himself. He's committed to trying new things. And he is fucking fearless.

Casey's life is a perfect example of one of my favorite maxims: You don't regret the things you do—only the things you *don't* do.

Real life is scary. It's hard. Knowing what you want—and taking those first steps to get it—requires guts, perseverance, and patience. It takes *courage* to face real life, because with every triumph (like Casey's) there are also failures. Every high has a low. Every peak comes with a valley. You get the point.

We tend to want to avoid those disappointments. Understandably! Who wants to try and fail? So we don't bother taking those first steps at all. We distract ourselves. We follow the easier path, the path of least resistance—spending more and more time on the Internet. Online, we can do everything that *feels* like living life—make "friends," explore culture, join a community—without ever having to look anyone in the eye.

But when we do that, we end up missing out on the potential of our lives.

————

I'm not saying that the Internet won't help you succeed. After all, it enabled Casey's success; he used it as a platform for his creativity. It worked. But not because he was using it as a *consumer*. Instead, he was a *creator*.

A consumer is someone who merely "likes" and shares things that other people make and post on social media sites; a creator, on the other hand, is someone who is generating that original material, whether they are a comedian tweeting jokes or a blogger uploading their own videos. Creators have an original voice, and the Internet is merely the outlet for that voice.

Casey was a perfect example of the latter. He was doing things offline, and then sharing them online. He had something real to contribute and promote—and *that's* the perfect use of the Internet. It's one of the reasons social media is great: It allows people like Casey to be heard in a way that they otherwise wouldn't. In the days before the Internet, Casey might never have been discovered or found a like-minded community of fans. Social media worked for him. It gave him a voice.

But, if you've read this far in the book (and hey, high five!), you know what I'm going to say next: As great as social media can be, it can also be a big, fat waste of time. Sure, the stuff we find online can be fascinating and inspiring, but every second that we spend on social media actually reduces the likelihood that we're going to do something ourselves. Surfing the Web and consuming other people's content in order to feel more connected and involved actually lowers our chances of making any kind of significant achievement of our own.

The truth is that the majority of people online aren't creators—although often we think that we are, because we are "involved." We get a false sense of fulfillment when we go online because we are participating in a community, but it's a one-sided exchange. By "liking" and reposting and commenting, we're not contributing in a significant way. There's an imbalance between input and outtake that teeters dangerously close to passivity.

Using the Internet is the simplest thing you can possibly do. Going online requires almost no energy. You can do it from your bed. In your underwear. Unshowered. It requires no commitment—after all, you can log out at any moment. It has no expectations of you, comes with zero accountability, and (in many cases) carries no repercussions for your actions when you use it.

There's no "failure" online, in the real-world sense—but there's no achievement, either. The things that seem like "success" online—gaining more friends; having people "like" your pictures, repost your comments, read your Twitter feed—are, for the most part, ephemeral. These social media achievements are merely a kind of popularity contest. And being popular online doesn't get us any closer to the things we want to achieve in real life. (I know there are exceptions—but they are not the norm.)

Think about someone you admire, someone you follow online who you really like. Then ask the question—why? Why is it that you like that person? I think you'll quickly realize that it's because they are actively *creating* something in the real world.

Personally, the two people I admire most online are Matthew Segal and Jarrett Moreno, the founders of OurTime.org, a nonprofit that is trying to give young people a political voice. They created the organization while they were at Kenyon College, after they observed their friends feeling disenfranchised during the 2004 elections—thanks to voting lines that were too long and convoluted registration laws, so many couldn't even vote. Matthew and Jarrett started a petition, then founded an organization, and now use social media and online organizing to help empower young people to understand political issues and act on them. They want to advocate on behalf of young Americans and effect real changes to benefit our collective future.

Matthew and Jarrett are heavily involved in social media—they tweet, post on Facebook, run a blog—but none of it is empty noise. They share meaningful information and relevant, current content, trying to help other people improve themselves. Social media is just another outlet for the things they are doing out there in the physical world.

(Similarly, supporting the creative content of people you truly admire by "liking" and retweeting their posts makes sense. This is how ideas get shared, and it is a constructive use of social media. Unfortunately, because it's so easy to click the "like" button, we are often too undiscerning in the things we share, and end up doing it mindlessly.)

> *Twitter provides us with a wonderful platform to discuss/confront societal problems. We trend Justin Bieber instead.*
>
> —Lauren Leto, comedian

The most popular things that people share online are the true-life, incredible experiences that only happen in the real world. Wouldn't *you* like to be the person having those experiences and mindfully sharing them, rather than simply capturing the low-hanging fruit and meaningless barrage of content that constantly comes at you?

So if, like me, you want to be more like Matthew, Jarrett, or Casey, start by making a list of your goals in life. Write down the things you'd really like to do—the dreams. How many of them are things you can accomplish simply by being online?

Life is filled with amazing and inspiring encounters. Instead of passively documenting them for the people you (barely) know online, I want to challenge you to absorb these moments and *do something* with them—become a writer, an artist, a dancer, a thinker. Learn skills that you'll have for the rest of your life. Travel. Explore. Grow. Advocate a political issue. Write a book. Take up a new hobby. Pursue that relationship. Try to do something new, and hard, and interesting.

You may fail—and yes, that will suck—but at least you will have tried. And who knows—instead of being a failure, you may be one of the successes. The only thing I can guarantee is that you won't be either if you don't give it a shot.

CHAPTER 21

Digital Detox

Hey, you.

Yes you, the one reading this book. I'm talking to you, okay?

I know what you're doing. You're reading this book, but in between pages you're picking up your phone and sending a text. You're refreshing your Facebook news feed. You're "liking" your friend's recent Instagram post and composing a tweet and checking your email for the twentieth time this hour.

It's time to step away from your computer. To put your phone somewhere you can't find it. To unplug and focus on the real world.

We—and when I say "we," I mean pretty much anyone under the age of forty—suffer from a compulsive need to share everything we are doing and seeing. We sleep with our phones next to our beds and look at them immediately when we wake up. We can't look at a sunset without Instagramming it. We can't eat a meal without taking a picture. We can't go to a movie without tweeting about it before the credits have even rolled. We almost feel guilty if we don't stay up-to-date on the twenty-four-hour nonstop feed. God forbid we miss something that everyone else is seeing and laughing about.

Let's just say it, okay? We are all totally addicted.

I'm not saying you shouldn't engage in social media at all—it *can* be incredibly rewarding, helping you connect with people you admire, keep up with friends, and express your opinions. I know you want to communicate; you have things to say! But all too often, we're forgetting to be participants in our own lives. After all, if you are constantly looking down at your phone, you're not interacting with the real world. Instead, you are distancing yourself by not being present.

Consider my friend Frank. I love him to death, but he drives me nuts. I cannot get him to put his phone down. He probably spends 75 percent of his working hours looking at his phone—checking social media feeds, looking at sports scores, texting with friends, reading emails. I'm sure he spends three or four hours a day looking at his phone—which, sadly, is just about normal for someone in their twenties.[24]

Frank makes it his goal to be super connected, but as a result, he lives in a state of incredible distraction. Every time we're together, I feel like he's more involved with the three people he's texting, or with his hundreds of Facebook friends, or with his thousand Twitter followers, than he is with me, who is standing right in front of him. He's so busy Instagramming a photo of where he is that he can't even enjoy what he's seeing.

Like Frank, we are all growing more distant from the experiences right in front of us. And it's not making us happier—in fact, exactly the opposite.

A recent study at the University of Michigan tracked the moment-to-moment happiness levels of college students throughout their days. The result? The more the students were on Facebook, the less happy they were. The moments when they were using social media were the moments when they had the most dissatisfaction with their own lives.[25] Enough said.

———

I recently asked my Facebook followers, "Do you feel like you spend too much time on your phone instead of engaging with the world around you?" The answer was a resounding yes. These were some of my favorite responses.

Jessica: My boyfriend is constantly on his phone.... When we're out to dinner it feels like I'm there alone.

Lauren: I literally just finished scrolling down Twitter and moved on to Facebook. There should be a social network rehab.

Korbin: I spend all day, whether working or enjoying leisure time, hovering over my fucking mobile. It's equal parts obsession and curse, but the way I look at it is that someday when I'm old and wrinkled I'm going to enjoy knowing that I have such a detailed account of my youth. It seems like a waste to some people but I almost find it liberating because it's a living archive of my time on this big rock. That being said sometimes even I annoy myself with how many times I log on to FB/Twitter/Insta. #dilemma

Nissa: I have a rule. When I am in the [presence] of company, phone is away. If my friends don't show the same respect for our time, I speak up and say something.

Katie: Honestly, I miss flip phones. I miss when you could go on dates and the only thing you could do was look at each other, and talk.

Lindsey: I constantly check my phone or my laptop...I feel like some of my friends & I have grown apart because we spend so much time talking on Facebook or texting... instead of making plans to hang out in person. Pretty sad... I'm ready to start connecting with people face to face again.

Since becoming kinda famous, I've experienced firsthand how people don't engage with the individuals and objects that interest them anymore: All they do is document things in order to share them online. For example, almost every day someone recognizes me and approaches me. But, without fail, I end up confused and disappointed by what happens next.

The person will say something like, "Oh my God! I'm such a big fan! Can I take a picture with you?" And without waiting for a response, they'll snap their picture and then flee, texting and uploading their photo immediately.

I'm left thinking, "That's it? You're a fan, you love my show, you have the opportunity to engage with me, and all you want is to take a picture to post to your Instagram? All you care about is showing people that you stood next to me for three seconds?"

I'm not a Madame Tussauds wax sculpture. Sure, if all you want is a picture, absolutely, take it. But don't be shy. Say something to me! Introduce yourself! Ask me a question! Let's have a conversation about the issues that we address on the show!

Surely that's more interesting and important than tweeting to your friends that I'm on your flight.

———

Let me lay out a familiar scenario for you. You're at a concert. The band has just started. What's the first thing you do? Take out your camera and take a picture, of course. Then you have to fiddle with that photo, worry about the exposure, and go in and out of applications, all before uploading it to Instagram. Maybe you even decide to record the performance, and end up watching the whole show through the two-inch screen on your smartphone. As a result, you're completely distracted during the entire concert.

These days, everyone is a photographer. We take photos and videos constantly, maxing out our hard drives, filling up our social feeds. It's so easy! After all, we all walk around with a camera in our pocket, thanks to the smartphone.

Photography, in its ideal use, is an art form, a way of capturing things that are important to you and saving them for the future. You shouldn't take pictures for other people; you should take them for yourself. But these days, we feel pressure to constantly take and upload photos for other people. Think about it. How many times have you thought: "I think this will get a lot of 'likes,'" or "That looks cool—I bet other people will think so, too," or "I want to film this concert so everyone knows I was here!"? It's not really about being inspired or memorializing a moment, is it? Instead, it ends up being something closer to bragging. Plus, on behalf of everyone behind you at the event, please know how distracting and irritating it is having your phone blocking my view the whole show.

Our default procedure, anytime we go to any event, is to take that camera out and start taking pictures. It's as if capturing the moment and sharing it later on is more valuable than actually *being there*. Without the proof that you were there, uploaded for other people's approval, your experience somehow doesn't count.

So before you whip out your phone, ask yourself this question: If what you are doing is so cool and so great that you want to take a picture, then why are you on your phone doing something else?

I'm not down on photography, of course. I'm a photographer by profession. For years, I lugged around my camera equipment everywhere I went. But it's all about intention. If you snap a single photo of a moment because you want to remember it, awesome. If you're taking pictures for a bigger purpose—an art project, your profession—and because you're inspired, then great. But if you're taking pictures just because you want to get recognition on social media? For the sole purpose of saying, "I was here"? Maybe it's time to rethink your intentions.

Photographers are, by definition, observers. Their job is to capture. And taking pictures is a second-degree activity. You are one layer removed from the action: You're literally looking through something. You're not seeing what you're looking at, because you're worried about framing and angles and process. If you're trying to enjoy yourself, taking pictures is a surefire way to ruin that. Trust me—I've taken a lot of photos. You can't have an immersive experience with a camera in front of your face.

In fact, you may not even clearly remember the experience at all. There was a fascinating recent study by a researcher at Fairfield University. He gave students digital cameras and then took them to an art museum, telling them to photograph some objects and simply observe others. The next day, the students were given a recall test. It turned out that they had far clearer memories of the things they *hadn't* photographed but had simply observed. As for the other objects? It seemed that subconsciously the students were counting on their photos to "remember" things for them, so they turned their brains off.[26]

If you go to a concert because you enjoy the music, then

you shouldn't be photographing or videorecording it. That's not your job. I can't say that there isn't something wonderful about the ability to capture and share culture on the Internet. It's an amazing thing. But your video of that song at that concert that you took with your phone from the nosebleed seats— the video where the stage is washed out and you can barely make out what the song is because the sound is so bad? Trust me, it isn't going to be as good as the music video the band has already made.

I'm guilty of doing this, too. It's hard to avoid in the culture that we live in. If I want to take really good pictures, I'll bring my real camera with me. I *like* to take photographs, especially at special events. But I struggle with this, because I know that I'm distracted when I photograph, and my enjoyment diminishes. So more and more I'm choosing to not take my camera.

I still bring my phone, though—it's unavoidable. And as long as it's in my pocket, I feel pressure to take pictures, because I have a following of people who want to see what I see. But every time I pull it out to take a picture, I know that it's not as good as the real thing. Not even close. It's a watered-down, miniature, low-res version of what's out there.

So lately, when I see something great and my first instinct is to take a picture with my phone, I take a minute to consider whether it's something I really need to photograph and whether my picture of what I'm seeing will even come close to capturing how great it is. Is my photograph going to be meaningful? Will it add value? Or will it be a sad reproduction of the moment? I find myself thinking, more and more, *I don't need to capture this—for me or for anyone else. It happened; I saw it. And that's good enough.*

So put that camera back in your pocket. Don't worry about sharing the moment with the people who aren't there. Just enjoy it.

———

But let's be honest, here—you're alive, and that means you probably have a smartphone, and you're probably pretty hooked on it. (Who isn't?) And I'm telling you to turn it off, to get off Instagram and Twitter and Facebook, to stop texting and tweeting and taking pictures. To step away from your computer and go out into the real world.

Easier said than done, right?

I don't have the easy, pain-free solution to unplugging. It would be amazing if I did. The truth is that we don't "go online" anymore, not the way we used to. The Internet is pervasive: We are constantly connected, through apps and social media and our phones. Technology is our life source, with no separation between online and offline. So sure, I can tell you to just turn off your phone, but we all know that isn't going to happen so easily.

So what's the answer? I have a fantasy about creating the perfect app, one that everyone would have preinstalled on their smartphone. The phone would lock you out until you engaged with one of thousands of different questions and suggestions—like "Do you really need to be sending a text right now?" or "Take a picture of something that inspires you, but don't share it with anyone else," or "Call your mom." The goal would be to make you think before you mindlessly tweeted/texted/commented/uploaded.

The app would also monitor how much time you spent online and what other apps you used—and it would cut you off when you were going overboard. You could set your own limits, and the phone would send you alerts: "You've spent 50 percent of your allotted time on Facebook." And if you felt like you were getting sucked into using certain apps too much, you could temporarily lock them out of your phone.

I haven't written that perfect app, but there are similar programs that already exist. The software programs Freedom and SelfControl both cut off all access to the Internet for a period of time that you set yourself; Anti-Social is a similar app, one that simply disables social media sites. RescueTime audits how much time you're spending on different apps and programs, giving you a graph of where you're wasting your time and how often you're switching between tasks. It's a kind of wake-up call.

But there are lots of ways you can work to reduce the impact of social media in your life without having to download an app to do it.

NEV'S RULES FOR SOCIAL MEDIA:

1. Start by turning your phone off. No, not forever—I know that's not going to happen. I'm talking about doing it for just twenty-four hours. Maybe you've already heard of the concept of a "Tech Sabbath"; if you haven't, the idea is to turn off your technology entirely for one day a week. Why not try it, at least once? Make it your challenge to yourself to leave your phone at home on Sundays. Make your plans the night before. Let your phone get some rest.

2. Set a new rule for yourself: If you are with someone, the phone stays in your pocket. Unless you are taking a photo or receiving an important cell phone call, *put away your phone*. No texts, no tweets, no email. Only use it when you are alone.

3. Set limits for yourself regarding social media. How many times a day do you currently post? Cut that number in half. No one needs to be posting ten or twenty times a day.

4. If you take photos at an event, don't post them to Instagram until you get home. Wait until the event is over, and *then* go through your photos to pick the one or two that you think are best. Be mindful in your choices.

5. Stop accepting friend requests from people you don't know! I'm not saying no new friends, but maybe you should consider more seriously whether you need to bring more strangers into your life.

6. Similarly, go through your friend list. If you don't know somebody personally, even if you have mutual friends, it's time to delete them. Fewer friends means less time spent catching up on news feeds.

7. When you feel compelled to text someone, stop and think. Why don't you call them instead? Have a real conversation—trust me, you'll get things accomplished a lot faster. While you're on the phone, ask them how they're doing. Make a plan to get together in person.

8. Every time you take out your phone to take a picture of a stranger, stop yourself. Go up to them instead and start a conversation. Ask a question. Find a way to engage with the people and things that catch your inter-

est beyond passively snapping a picture. Who knows what you might learn?

9. Similarly, instead of relying on your phone when you need directions or advice, go up to actual human beings and ask for help.

10. Start a No Phones at the Dinner Table rule. Some restaurants have already started to do this; why not apply it in your home, too?

11. Buy an alarm clock. The real kind. That way you won't feel so compelled to plug your phone in next to your bed at night. Leave it overnight in another room, instead.[27]

In his great book *Outliers*, Malcolm Gladwell lays out the "10,000-hour rule." Basically, in ten thousand hours you can become a master at almost any task: Become a chess champion, an NBA-worthy basketball player, a best-selling novelist. It seems like a Sisyphean task, right?

Well, with the average person spending three hours a day on social media—or far more, if you include all forms of Internet use—that's a *minimum* of one thousand hours a year. If you cut out social media entirely, with the time you saved you could be a Gladwell-style master at something in less than ten years.

Okay, yes, ten years is a long time. But what if you gained just a few months of time? What could you accomplish with that?

- Take up exercise and lose twenty pounds.
- Become a really good cook.
- Learn a new language.

- Master the guitar.
- Read ten great books.
- Train for and run a half marathon.
- Take classes in art, photography, writing—anything you can think of.
- Get to know someone new really well.

If it's making you truly happy, sure, go ahead and keep your phone in your hand and your eyes on it all the time. But if you're like me and want a life of experience and adventure and amazement (and I bet you do), put that thing away. There's no life in your phone. Life is what happens when you're *not* looking down at what you're holding in your hands. The smartphone is just a way to capture and share it.

Instead, invest in creating the content of your life. This will endure long after your last tweet has come and gone.

CHAPTER 22

Fame Fail

I grew up believing that movie stars had it easy. I'd look at someone like Leonardo DiCaprio and think that his life was a piece of cake. Someone had put him in a movie, and now he was set: He was rich, famous, and dating beautiful women. Wouldn't it be awesome if that happened to me? Maybe it could. It would probably solve all my problems. That was my impression of celebrity: It just *happens* to you. It's just the luck of the draw.

We live in a world where people are obsessed with celebrity. Like me, people think that fame is a matter of luck; that it can happen to anyone. Just take a look at the people on reality TV! We fixate on this. And as a result, it's getting in the way of our ability to live our lives.

In an increasingly overpopulated, underemployed society, we've shifted our focus away from traditional work ethic ideals and toward tabloid celebrity ideals. We used to believe that hard work paid off; now, we focus on easy fame. As a society, we center all our attention on a tiny segment of people who, frequently for no good reason, have been able to make truckloads of money doing nothing. Kids today dream of being a Bachelor/ette, a Real Housewife, a member of the Kardashian family, or an American Idol.

I get it. Real-world options are pretty bleak for a lot of people. Option A, the best-case scenario, for so many young people around the world? You get to take on a tremendous amount of work and debt in order to educate yourself, with the relatively low chance of getting a good job; and even if you do get that job, you'll have to work incredibly hard for decades in order to earn an at-best modest living, a lot of which will go to pay off your student loans and the rest of which will (hopefully) let you live in a semidecent house and support a family—eventually retiring in your seventies, if you're lucky.

Nope, it's not sexy. The middle-class norm has become a dream. That's why fame has become such an alluring idea, and why everyone fantasizes about option B: becoming a reality TV star. Young people look at the cast of *Duck Dynasty*—all *they* had to do was be extreme versions of themselves while the cameras rolled, and for that they made a couple hundred thousand dollars an episode. Just for hanging out. And being obnoxious.

We, as a culture, have elevated that. We've made it a worthy goal. Because it requires so little talent and effort, we believe it's an option within anyone's reach.

As difficult as it might seem to achieve option A, the odds of option B are worse than winning the lottery. As one of the few people who has (incredibly) won that lottery, I can give you the inside scoop: Most people on reality TV shows don't get paid a lot. In fact, most hardly get paid anything at all. Even if you do miraculously get cast in a reality TV show, there's a very small chance it will make it to a pilot, a smaller chance that the pilot will get picked up by a TV channel, and an even tinier chance that the show will make it past two episodes. And even if you are in that infinitesimal number that makes it all the way to season 2, you still won't make much money because of the standard contract you signed back in season 1.

Sure, should your show become one of the 2 percent of all TV shows that are smash hits, you'll make some money. Best-case scenario? The money will last for a couple years. I guarantee that you won't end up a millionaire and retire at age thirty unless you have an unbelievable business manager. Instead, you'll be a has-been reality star with an empty bank account and no skills worth mentioning.

You might be thinking, "But even if I don't make a ton of money, it's still a glamorous lifestyle!" Not exactly. Though I am not Brad Pitt, I can speak to the fact that hosting a reality TV show and being something of a celebrity does not make for a dazzling day-to-day experience. While I feel incredibly lucky to be doing what I do, I want to be honest with you. Being a public figure generally involves a lot of long airplane flights, early mornings, hard work, and very little time spent with friends and family.

Option A may be the less sexy option, but if you go to college you're improving yourself. You're growing. You're opening yourself up to the world, ideas, and people that will excite you.

As I travel for the show, I meet with a lot of young people who have a bleak outlook on life. "I come from a small town, a middle- or lower-class family," they'll say. "Maybe I can go to a community college or state school and not rack up too much debt. But then what do I do?" Or they'll tell me, "I don't plan to go to college, so I'll just get a job in my town, doing construction or working in fast food. That's life."

But people don't realize how many different kinds of careers are out there, how many truly amazing, interesting things you can do. Some may require college degrees, but a lot require only self-motivation and drive. We only focus on the top 1 percent of people who are crazy successful in their fields, the people whose names are recognizable to us. Pop culture doesn't really highlight all the other people whose behind-the-scenes jobs are critical in those same industries.

So you're into fashion? Don't aspire to be on *Project Runway* or *Fashion Star*. Instead, learn as much as you can about fashion and become a stylist or a personal shopper. Or you're into movies? Instead of focusing on being a movie star, think about all the other great jobs in the movie industry. Start as a production assistant, get an internship, or become a makeup artist or production designer or grip. There are so many possibilities!

Or you're really into social media? Make that addiction work for you. There are so many jobs in marketing these days. Companies are desperate for social media page managers. Mock up a Facebook page for a local business that's not online, then go in and show them. Offer to run it for them for free. See if you like it, and if you do, go to another business and say, "I've been doing this for another company and I'll do it for you for a hundred dollars a week." And then you've got a portfolio and you can go to another company, and then another. In a matter of months, you might find yourself with a full-time job running a company's social media campaign.

Make your own opportunities. Remember how I was really into dance when I was young? I recognized early on that I was never going to be a famous ballet dancer. As much as I loved dance, I just wasn't star material; I didn't have the abilities or talent required. So few people do. But I knew I wanted to be involved in that world somehow, so I found a place for myself taking photographs instead. I offered my services for free for a long time, just making myself indispensable. Eventually, I found myself making a living as a ballet videographer. I paved my own path, found a goal that was achievable, and went for it.

———

There's a big misconception that things just *happen* in life—that fame will find you if you're fabulous. But things only happen to you when you are out living life. Your prospects are only as good as you make them.

The reason most people (outside of reality TV stars) are famous is because they *do* things. That actor you love from that TV show worked really hard to learn how to act. He struggled through countless auditions and callbacks to get a shitty part that led to a less shitty part that led, eventually, to an okay part... you get the point. He *earned* every second of screen time he got. *That's* why people get famous. *That's* why people succeed. It wasn't just the luck of the draw, as I once believed.

The world needs more doers.

Good news! Most people are too busy worrying about the "likes" on their Instagram feed and followers on Twitter to actually be out there doing stuff. The fact that you are reading this book and not just looking at your phone means that you want to think, engage, and participate in life. You've got a head start.

So if you're reading this right now and, in the back of your mind, are thinking that there's something you wish you were doing, a job you'd like to have... *go do it*. You'll have a jump start.

As for the fame that so many people think will solve all their problems? Let me tell you, as someone who has experienced it—it's not all that. Don't get me wrong; I feel extremely grateful and humbled every day by my job. But it doesn't make me any happier. If anything, it adds pressure and anxiety—because now there are expectations. I have to be "always on."

Nothing gets fixed simply because you are on a TV show. No number in a bank account is going to help you with your girlfriend. You are not going to be magically happier if you have a million Twitter followers instead of ten. Your issues will always be your issues, until you address them.

CHAPTER 23

Put On a Smiley Face

*S*tay positive.

If you were to ask me to sum up everything I've learned since I was first contacted by Angela almost seven years ago, that's what I'd say. Embrace who you really are, both online and off; improve yourself if you don't like what you see. Try to remain optimistic. And learn how to create a good thing out of whatever life throws at you.

I know, I know, I'm not the first person to say any of this. But I think it bears repeating, ad nauseam, thanks to the state of the world we are currently living in.

We live in an online society of "likes." Social media culture is all about wanting to be loved. We want our Instagrams to be liked, our tweets to be retweeted, our comments to be reposted. Our public lives are our most intimate work of art, and we want only positive reviews of the curated self-portrait that we depict there, all day, every day.

It's an extremely unrealistic hope.

People have been weird and crazy and negative and afraid for a long time—think about the Salem Witch Trials or the Spanish Inquisition—but social media has really generated an epidemic of unhappiness. The outcome of living a life in public, on social media, is that we are not only battling our own loneliness and discontent but making ourselves susceptible to other lonely and discontent people who take their emotions

out on us and try to bring us down for daring to reveal ourselves. Unhappy people who will look at that meticulously
curated life and give it a bad review. Whether we like it or not,
when we live our lives online we have to be prepared to cope
with all this cynicism.

> *Try being informed instead of just opinionated.*
> —Anonymous

So what can you do about it?

We all have to be careful about allowing negativity to
enter our minds, in any dosage. It affects us. Sure, it's good
to be exposed to a diversity of opinions. But it's a waste of
time to seriously consider the negative feelings of someone
who means nothing to you—someone who is not important
in your life and who in all likelihood you will never meet. You
should never let that person dictate how you feel.

Because here's the thing about negativity: It in no way
helps you. Every moment you spend being negative or
angry has zero value. No product or achievement or success
comes from negativity. It just wastes your time and gets in
your way.

———

When the documentary *Catfish* came out, in 2010, most
of the attention it received was incredibly supportive and
wonderful. But not long after the movie's release, the negative fallout began. Certain online reviews called Rel, Henry,
and me "rich, spoiled New York City kids" and accused us of
exploiting my catfish, Angela, and her family. (That couldn't
have been farther from the truth.) Posters on online bulletin

boards called us liars and claimed that we'd faked the movie. Across the Internet, people were downright mean.

It tore me apart. These strangers were calling me exploitative and dishonest. But I'd never had a more real experience in my life. I lived it. I knew it was true. It was *crazy* to me that they didn't believe me. I let it get to me. Instead of feeling great about having helped make this fascinating and successful documentary, I began to feel depressed.

Finally, Andrew Jarecki—our producer, and a great documentary filmmaker himself (if you haven't seen *Capturing the Friedmans*, you should)—said something that really woke me up. As he read through the bad reviews, his response was, "This is great for us. Because if everyone liked something, it would be boring."

In other words, he spun the negativity into something positive: If Rel, Henry, and I were getting people enamored and excited—but also riled up and upset—it meant we'd done something right. When you succeed creatively, Jarecki continued, you will *always* run into people who will spin your success against you because they are dealing with their own issues.

Rel, Henry, and I had caught lightning in a bottle. We had busted our butts making a movie out of a true life experience that was incredibly unusual. But we ran into a lot of luck—luck not only that I had the experience but also that my brother was a filmmaker who happened to start filming what was going on. Luck that my catfish agreed to be in the movie. Luck that we hooked up with amazing producers who helped us get our film into Sundance. A million things had to happen to make the movie, all of which were hard to believe.

I realized that a lot of the film's critics, aspiring to artistic achievements of their own, saw our luck and success and were annoyed. They didn't want to believe our film, because by believing in what we'd done, they had to question their inability to achieve their own dreams. And that pissed them off, so they chose to tear us down instead.

Understanding this, I had a revelation: I *knew* what had happened to me. I was there. So as weird and frustrating and difficult as it was that these people online didn't believe me—who cared? These haters were making up their minds to feel a certain way because of who *they* were, not who I was. If they had the ambition to actually find out the truth, they could have—but they didn't want to. There was nothing I could do about that.

So I let it go. I decided that these strangers weren't worth worrying about. Instead, I accepted the simple truth that I couldn't control what other people thought. All I could do was try not to let it get to me, and channel that hate into something more productive.

After the *Catfish* backlash, I decided to use my experience as motivation to think about how I could use my platform to peacefully spread *positivity.* For the first time, I started really considering everything I posted on the Internet and how it could be perceived. I identified the morals and ideals that I wanted to be associated with and made sure that everything I said or posted was furthering those messages. I resisted the urge to post things that were snarky or even just mindlessly funny; I didn't want to be a curator of entertainment. I wanted to be someone who stood for real content and value.

The surprising thing that I discovered? People felt that positivity and returned it. By channeling my frustration into something more fruitful, I not only helped other people feel better, but also ultimately I felt better about myself.

———

When I was younger, I used to notice only the negative things around me. Stupid, silly things: people who walked too slowly, bad drivers, red lights. Anger became an outlet for my emotional energy—something I could identify and understand, as opposed to the murky feelings of negative self-doubt that I dealt with every day. And as a result, I ended up spending a lot of time and energy being angry, missing out on and ignoring things that were great and would have made me happy.

That's why, lately, I've been trying to change my perspective. It's the battle I'm actively fighting: Rather than noticing something I don't like or getting upset about a nasty comment I read, I now try to acknowledge the negativity and look elsewhere for something that *does* make me happy. I remind myself how much good there is in the world, how nice someone was to me today, how lucky I am. Even simple things, like great weather or the fact that I ate a meal and have a full belly, can help boost my mood.

I've noticed that doing this has an immediate effect on me. When you work hard at noticing positivity and good fortune, your brain and heart feel better. And when you start to feel better and think better, you perform better. Everything improves.

So I'll say it one last time: *Stay positive.*

You've heard that line a million times before, I know. It makes you want to roll your eyes. It's not that easy, you think. You have physical issues, pain and sickness; emotional stress; problems with friends and family. There are haters everywhere you turn, giving you negative feedback, saying nasty things. And in the middle of all that you need to make money, find love, build a life. It's hard enough just to survive, let alone be upbeat about it.

And yet, everything good in life ties back to the idea of positivity. If you're struggling with something—a relationship problem, a work crisis, friendship drama—take a moment to recognize how you feel, assess what you want, and then approach the problem using a positive thought process. If you do, you'll be far likelier to resolve the situation than if you march in pissed off and pessimistic.

It's easy to get discouraged or bogged down. But keep your focus on the positive and on what you truly stand for, and know that what you're doing is what you're *supposed* to be doing.

Conclusion

Even though Rel, Henry, and I coined the term *catfish* with our documentary, we never really intended the term to refer to someone who lies about their identity online.

During my stay in Michigan, Angela's husband, Vince, told me this amazing story. Fisheries used to ship these giant vats of live cod from Alaska to China, but they kept running into a problem. Upon arrival in China, the cod's flesh was mushy and tasteless from the fish being inactive on the journey. So some guy had the bright idea to put catfish in the vats with the cod to chase them around and keep them moving.

When Vince finished telling me this story, I knew that's what Angela had been to me—a catfish of sorts, who had kept me intrigued, eased my loneliness, made me feel like I had finally maintained a great relationship. She had gotten my blood moving and had been a catalyst of sorts.

It's time to redefine *catfish* in a more positive light: someone who breaks the rules and figures out new ways to do things. Someone who inspires, rather than deceives. Someone who keeps us intrigued—for the right reasons rather than the wrong ones. Let's *all* be catfish.

The world needs leaders that can guide us on matters both big—how to deal with the financial crisis around the world, how to fight hunger, or how to preserve our planet—and seemingly small—how to use Facebook in a more moral way, or how to implement a society based on positivity. There's no reason you—yes, *you*—can't be that leader.

You don't think you're ready to be a leader? Then be a follower. There's a great TED Talk by musician/entrepreneur Derek Sivers about how movements get started. He shows footage of a guy at an outdoor concert—the *only* guy who is dancing, and in a really goofy way. Everyone else stands and laughs at him. And then one person, maybe on a dare, goes over and starts mock goofy dancing with him. And then two other people go over, and then five, and suddenly the *entire lawn* is dancing. It's practically a mosh pit.[28]

That first dancer, the leader, was critical, but just as important? The first guy who joined him. Being a follower can be just as daring and courageous—because once a leader has a follower, that's when a movement can start to happen. And every member of a movement is critical.

Regardless of who you are, remember this: You are an important and a crucial part of the future. Your ideas and actions can change the world—you can inspire a thousand people to change the way they think. You could help start a revolution, like the first person in Egypt who was brave enough to speak up in protest and helped start the Arab Spring. Don't be afraid to be that person. As Bruce Springsteen once said, you can't start a fire without a spark.

The Internet can suck, but it can also be great if we use it right and harness its powers for meaningful change. You can be one of the creators, using social media to distribute groundbreaking new work and ideas that alter our social fabric. Find something you believe in, something meaningful, and let that consciously inform your life, both offline and on.

So my final challenge to you? Get out of your chair and

go out and change the world. We need people to set the tone and guide us, because now more than ever there's an opportunity for new and better direction. Don't make your goal to be liked on Facebook. Make it to stand for something. You may not feel as popular at first, but believing in something and sticking to it is what makes life meaningful. And personal meaning is at the foundation of self-respect, of confidence, and—ultimately—of love.

Acknowledgments

I would never have been able to write this book if it hadn't been for the unconditional love and support of my family. I can only imagine the heartaches and headaches I must have caused you over the years. You taught me how to be kind, humble, generous, and expressive. You encouraged my creativity and applauded my individuality. If every kid could experience the love and positivity that I received from my family, I know the world would be a better place.

I also want to thank Angela Wesselman-Pierce. Somehow our paths through this crazy universe ended up crossing and I am grateful every day that they did. I appreciate your courage. I admire your commitment and I recognize your creativity. Thank you for sharing your story with me.

I could not have written this book without the guidance and support of Janelle Brown. You are a wonderful writer, trusted confidant, and good friend.

I want to thank my brother, Rel, and my brother-from-another-mother Henry for being my role models, both personally and professionally. I couldn't ask for a better pair of gentlemen to call my best friends.

Of course it goes without saying that much of my success is a result of the talent and intelligence of Max Joseph. There isn't anybody I'd rather be out there with, and I can't express how much of a positive influence your advice and companionship has had on me.

To my representation, who has had to put up with me and my passionate frustrations and constant queries since the beginning: Thank you for believing in me and helping me navigate the murky waters of this business.

Thanks to the entire team at Hachette / Grand Central Publishing, starting with Pippa White for taking a chance on a first-time writer with nothing but a gut feeling that we were on to something. And for all the hard work of Sonya Cheuse, Jamie Snider, Brigid Pearson, Brian McLendon, Andrew Duncan, Jane Lee, Beth de Guzman, and Jamie Raab.

Shanee. No words can describe the intense feeling of satisfaction knowing that there is somebody on this planet who gets me. I feel loved. I feel needed. You give me purpose and I can't wait to share our lives together. I love you.

And finally, to all my friends throughout the years: Thank you for giving me a chance. Thank you for giving me a second chance and often many more chances after that. I know it took a while, but all of you played a part and made a huge difference in helping me become who I am today.

Notes

1. http://www.youtube.com/watch?v=s-CTkbHnpNQ
2. http://mashable.com/2010/10/14/nielsen-texting-stats/
3. http://www.economist.com/node/16660401; http://www
   .digitaltrends.com/social-media/facebook-could-be-larger
   -than-china-in-three-years-time/#!JOQrc
4. MTV "Millennials" survey.
5. *Noah,* Toronto Film Festival. Available online at http://www
   .fastcocreate.com/3017108/you-need-to-see-this-17-minute
   -film-set-entirely-on-a-teens-computer-screen
6. http://www.cnn.com/2012/05/04/tech/social-media/
   facebook-lies-privacy/
7. http://www.womansday.com/sex-relationships/dating-marriage/
   online-dating-profile-lies
8. http://www.dailybulletin.com/general-news/20130517/sexting
   -probe-leads-to-arrest-at-rancho-etiwanda-high-schools, http://
   losangeles.cbslocal.com/2013/05/09/students-face-possible
   -child-porn-charges-in-sexting-scandal/
9. http://www.cnn.com/2013/09/27/us/miss-teen-usa-sextortion/
10. http://www.seattleweekly.com/home/933841-129/
    crimepunishment
11. http://www.mcafee.com/us/about/news/2013/q1/20130204-01
    .aspx
12. http://www.cnn.com/2013/08/22/us/florida-fraternity-facebook/

13. http://www.jsonline.com/news/crime/greenfield-teens-facebook
-post-for-drugs-leads-to-arrest-131826718.html

14. http://www.cbsnews.com/news/baby-with-bong-facebook
-photo-arrest-fla-mom-rachel-stieringer-faces-drug-charges/

15. http://www.dailymail.co.uk/news/article-1206491/Woman
-sacked-Facebook-boss-insult-forgetting-added-friend.html

16. http://www.huffingtonpost.com/2010/07/26/fired-over-facebook
-posts_n_659170.html

17. http://www.nytimes.com/2013/08/08/us/broader-sifting-of-data
-abroad-is-seen-by-nsa.html?pagewanted=all&_r=3&

18. http://www.themevision.com/files/clark%20v%20indiana%20
admissibility%20MySpace%20page%20evidence.pdf

19. http://fort-greene.thelocal.nytimes.com/2009/11/11/
his-facebook-status-now-charges-dropped/?_r=0

20. http://www.match.com/magazine/article/4671/

21. http://www.nydailynews.com/life-style/one-third-u-s-marriages
-start-online-dating-study-article-1.1362743

22. MTV "Millennials" survey.

23. http://www.youtube.com/watch?v=WsYAXPqVnYM

24. http://www.marketingcharts.com/wp/interactive/social
-networking-eats-up-3-hours-per-day-for-the-average-american
-user-26049/

25. http://drdeepikachopra.com/the-well-list-1/social-media-dis
-connection

26. http://www.theatlanticcities.com/technology/2013/12/how
-camera-phones-modify-our-memories/7829/

27. Thank you to Deepika Chopra for the last three ideas in our list.
http://www.mindbodygreen.com/0-10977/10-tips-to-spend-less
-time-on-social-media-more-time-with-humans.html

28. http://www.ted.com/talks/derek_sivers_how_to_start_a
_movement.html

I finally met "Megan" from the photos.
(Me and Aimee Gonzales.)